A Fig at the Gate

Other books by Kate Llewellyn

Novel
Dear You

Journal
The Waterlily: A Blue Mountains Journal
The Mountain
Burning: A Journal
Playing with Water: A Story of a Garden

Autobiography
The Dressmaker's Daughter

Travel
Angels and Dark Madonnas: Travels in India and Italy
Lilies, Feathers and Frangipani
Gorillas, Tea and Coffee: An African Sketchbook

Poetry
Trader Kate and the Elephants
Luxury
Honey
Figs
Selected Poems
Crosshatched
Sofala and Other Poems
Poets and Perspectives: Kate Llewellyn with Essays by David Gilbey, Susan
Sheridan and Anne Collett

Essays
The Floral Mother and Other Essays

Edited
The Penguin Book of Australian Women Poets (co-editor with Susan
Hampton)

Letters
As You May Already Know: Selected Letters of Kate Llewellyn 1997–2004,
edited by Ruth Bacchus and Barbara Hill

A Fig at the Gate

KATE LLEWELLYN

The joys of friendship, gardening
and the gaining of wisdom

ALLEN&UNWIN
SYDNEY • MELBOURNE • AUCKLAND • LONDON

First published in 2014
This edition published in 2016

Australian Government

This project has been assisted by
the Australian Government through
the Australia Council for the Arts,
its arts funding and advisory body.

Allen & Unwin
83 Alexander Street
Crows Nest NSW 2065
Australia
Phone: (61 2) 8425 0100

Email: info@allenandunwin.com
Web: www.allenandunwin.com

Cataloguing-in-Publication details are available
from the National Library of Australia
www.trove.nla.gov.au

ISBN 978 1 76029 256 0

Cover and internal design by Lisa White

Set in 12/17 pt Fairfield LH by Post Pre-press Group, Australia

Garden map by Geoff Wilson

Cover image: Hand-coloured lithograph of *Ficus carica* from *Darstellung und Beschreibung
sämtlicher in der Pharmacopoea Borusica aufgeführten offizinellen Gewächse* by Otto Carl Berg &
Carl Friedrich Schmidt offered by antiquarian book and print dealer Jan Meemelink
(www.meemelink.com).

Printed and bound in Australia by Griffin Press

10 9 8 7 6 5 4 3 2

To Joan Paroissien, Tarla Kramer and the late Dinah Ayers

' . . . a living dog is better than a dead lion.'
Ecclesiastes 9:4

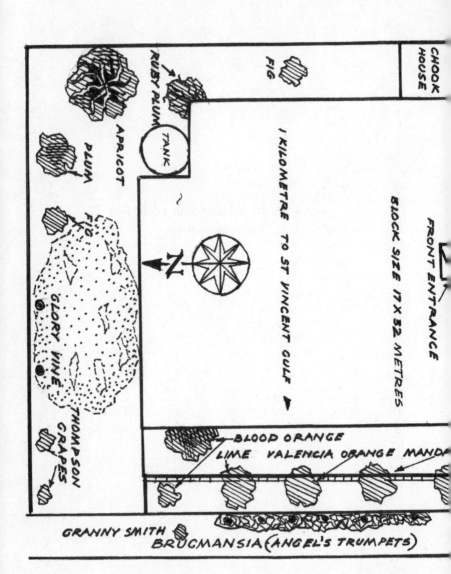

CHOOK HOUSE

FIG

RUBY PLUM

APRICOT

PLUM

FIG

TANK

1 KILOMETRE TO ST VINCENT GULF ▶

BLOCK SIZE 17 X 32 METRES

FRONT ENTRANCE

N

GLORY VINE

THOMPSON GRAPES

BLOOD ORANGE

LIME   VALENCIA   ORANGE   MANDA

GRANNY SMITH

BRUGMANSIA (ANGEL'S TRUMPETS)

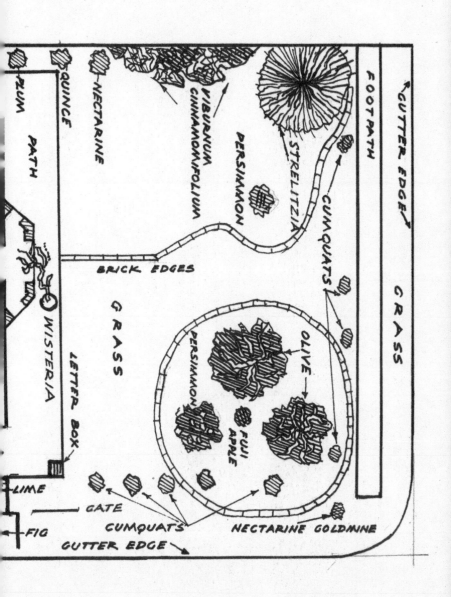

Contents

Prelude

It began in Patagonia in the lounge of a seedy hotel with floor to ceiling windows looking out onto roofs and nothing much else. Bored, two landscape gardeners were discussing how they would renovate the hotel. We had been on the road for a fortnight and were drinking pisco sours but our talk was running out. We were twenty Australians, often in a bus, looking at the famous gardens of Chile. Many were garden designers and others, like me, were amateur gardeners.

Knowing that these plans were only theories and feeling vaguely irritated because it showed we had run out of zeal, I thought it would be excusable to ask a professional question of them. So I did.

'I have bought a house and it needs a new garden. There's only a huge fifty-year-old strelitzia, a line of big agaves and three oleander trees in the front. What should I do?'

Immediately Suzanne looked up over her glass and said, 'I'd rip out the oleanders and plant a blue and orange garden to match the strelitzia.'

I blinked and knew at once that that was what I would do. I've made a few gardens in my time, although I didn't begin gardening until in my fifties.

Phillip Johnson stood up, offered us more pisco sours and said, 'I could send my team in, Kate, and we could make you a beautiful garden with a billabong.'

I said, 'Phill, I haven't got the means for anything that has the word "team" in it. But I'll have another drink, thanks.'

Next day, one of the women on the trip, Sue Forge, who has a famous garden in Melbourne called 'Freesia', said, on hearing of Suzanne's advice, 'Yes, and plant a cumquat hedge. And I'd grow wisteria over the verandah.'

Again, entranced, I meant to do it as soon as I moved into the house.

As we headed in a bus towards the Atacama Desert, I started planning the garden. It was apt that it was the Atacama, one of the driest places on earth, because drought is becoming more common in Adelaide. I thought of the plants I'd use to make my ideal garden, which is the opposite of groomed. I wanted it to look like a rough beard at the front of the house, with olives, and all the plants that old farmhouses in the north of the state had: white iris, lavender, plectranthus and Russian sage. I'd have no truck with roses, I've done my dash with them. Like curtains, we're through.

My three brothers, Tucker (Tom), Bill and Peter, have places in Adelaide and my nursing friends, with whom I trained at the Royal Adelaide Hospital fifty years ago, live nearby. I was lonely living near Wollongong because my friends were academics and we only saw each other on weekends. I decided to come home to die.

Also, because finding myself in old age, baffled, pleased and astonished, I thought it could be interesting to watch my friends and I grow old and chart the triumphs and disasters of our ageing. It could be a book about geometry. As the gardener shrinks in her ageing, the garden should expand. In the end, it will be all garden and no author.

Above all, I wanted to go back to having a garden that would feed me and my friends; back to what almost everyone had in their childhood, which was a garden that would partly sustain the family. One where I could hand a bucket of plums over the fence, and give away apricot jam; where there'd be herbs and tomatoes, spinach, kale and cabbages. To help water this garden, I took for granted that I could save water from the shower.

Having grown up with an average rainfall of 14 inches at Tumby Bay on Eyre Peninsula, across two gulfs from where my house is now, saving water was no hardship. In fact to squander it was upsetting.

Phillip Johnson, who'd been buying the pisco sours, and I watched some of the lavish waste of water in many of the great gardens in Chile. It streamed from hoses left running, forgotten perhaps. Water ran away in rivulets, in rills and gutters, and no one seemed to notice or care. 'They will though, one day,' Phillip said as we stood watching. (In 2013 Phillip and his team won the Chelsea Flower Show prize for 'Best in Show' for a billabong garden with water harvested from nearby roofs.)

The first autumn

The hedge is planted with gaps as there aren't enough cumquat trees available, the oleanders have gone and there are two curved beds, one with a persimmon tree and an orange tree and the other with two olives. This is a windy place. What I did not know then was that citrus hate wind. The garden is built on a corner site and the wind tears up from the beach a kilometre away and then can turn and belt down from the hills which overlook the city.

'I shall lift up mine eyes to the hills,' I thought.

Blue and sheltering, the hills are quarried for sandstone and bluestone with which this sweet city was built.

Autumn in Adelaide is sublime. I swim almost every day and the nights are cool and starry.

I needed a fence not only because dogs and people stroll across the garden but also because dogs have no consciousness of what I consider is my territory. They sniff around and dig up the compost I have trenched in around the trees. It is a curious thing, but having no fence makes me feel vulnerable living here alone, not that a fence would stop anybody who wanted to come to the door or window. But most of our feelings about safety are not rational: a window can be broken with a spade or a brick in a trice. An example of the fact that everything is only what we think about it: what we think or feel, however, is not necessarily true or rational.

Speaking of the rational, the lack of a front fence also means that people are able to discover me weeding or watering when I have had the foolish idea that I will just begin doing this one little thing which turns out to be a much bigger, longer thing. Not having intended to be seen, I was once startled to hear my neighbour, Karen, say as she passed while walking her black labrador which runs into my garden, 'Well, that's the first time I've ever seen anyone garden in a bike helmet!'

I had dismounted and decided to put in some plants which I'd just brought home from the nursery.

Any gardener will tell you that gardening in a dressing gown is one of life's simple pleasures. Sometimes I don't notice, having begun weeding when going out to fetch the paper from the lawn in my horrible pink dressing gown. I can't throw it away because it won't wear out and is warmer and quicker to dry than any other. The sheepskin slippers are getting muddy. I notice it when a passerby doesn't reply when I say, 'Good morning'. They quicken their step. Nightclothes worn during the day embarrasses some people. Yet in Kings Cross, which I admit Hove is not, they say that old women used to go down Macleay Street in their dressing gowns to fetch milk and the paper.

Old age liberates one from convention.

'Remember those old women we nursed who used to fling their

legs around?' said a friend, Mary Harrison, when she told me this theory of hers. At that time I did not think it would apply to me.

Down on the western side of the house there was a dry buffalo lawn beside a path. I did not have the strength to dig it out so I gathered barrow loads of newspapers from my brother Peter who lives nearby and laid them over the lawn. Then I asked Steve from Jim's Mowing if he would give me bags of his lawn clippings. He tipped out about ten huge bags, and another mower I accosted in the street gave me another eight. They were happy to do it: it saved them paying a fee to leave the grass at the rubbish dump. In fact, this is how I made the whole garden.

Over the next six months I planted a dozen or so various tomato plants into the clippings. Never having succeeded in growing any vegetables at all, the result was astounding to me. My grand-daughter, Claudia, who is unusually besotted with gardening (she was sending off mail orders from her own Tesselaar's cata-logue at eight), came to stay with her parents and her sister at Christmas. I suggested that she gather tomatoes so that we could make chutney. She took a bucket down to the side of the house and began to fill it. A sensible child, seeing the size of the crop, she abandoned the bucket and fetched the wheelbarrow. And it is not exaggerating to say that she half filled it and day after day she went back for more. We baked 'Tiny Tom' tomatoes on their stems in oil, salt and herbs and filled sterile jars with them (which later turned toxic).

We made both green tomato chutney and red chutney and still the bushes fruited. I left bags of tomatoes on the doorsteps of neighbours and made panzanella by the bucket load. In the end I was sick of tomatoes and longed for the bushes to die off. Then when they did, they still held ripening tomatoes which my Italian friend, Marisa, said her father used to hang up in his shed and keep for weeks or months over winter. But I piled them up and waited for them to turn to compost, which they never did. Ants ate the fruit and some seeds fell to the ground and now there are seedlings which fill me with hope.

One of the reasons the crop was so good was that I did not succeed in tying the plants onto stakes, though I tried with the aid of my friend Lindy's black stockings. They fell down and I left the plants lying there. In March, when we had fifteen straight days of more than 35 degrees, the tomatoes were hidden by leaves and the fallen branches had sent out roots, keeping the plants low, huge and sprawling. This meant that the fruit did not cook on the vine. Because of this experience, I will never stake tomatoes again.

Lindy is one of the nurses. She and her husband, Robert, live nearby. She's a walker. Four or five times a week, we take a 10-kilometre walk to Glenelg. While we walk, we talk. Our subjects are her hatred of the government, our brothers—hers are in the Barossa Valley as her parents began St Hallett winery. Also we talk of our other friends, meals we're planning, and books and death.

HARBOUR

When I first sailed into Sydney Harbour
I cried. A man standing, watching,
asked what was up.
'It's so beautiful,' I said.
And he replied, 'Oh to be so young.'

Now old, beauty no longer makes me cry.
Instead, from time to time, there are
glimpses of what else matters
and a chance to act.
While I can't erase what I did
there is the gift, the opportunity,
knowing that time is short
the little casual things
I didn't see turn into a roar
I no longer can ignore.

It is this, the chance of grace
that consoles my slowing pace.

2009

Winter

Saturday, 27 June

Oh! The glory of having no fruit fly! Those quarantine fruit bins on the sides of the roads coming into our state are shrines to me. I would kneel and light candles there. (People are asked to drop any fruit they have with them into the bins to guard against bringing in fruit fly and other pests.) Never before have I gardened where there is no fruit fly. No need to spray as my neighbour Terry had to do when I lived beside him at Woonona near Wollongong. It meant that if anybody was to have tomatoes without fruit fly, big poisons were needed. There was a line of poison sprayed in back-yards parallel with the line of Hills Hoists between Sydney and Wollongong.

It's getting dark at five o'clock. I take dinner on a tray to bed and enjoy myself. No one around to judge.

Sunday, 19 July

I picked yellow roses from my sister-in-law Helen's garden to take to Aunty Beck who is 103 and in Resthaven at Norwood. She is a happy woman. 'Oh Kate, I can see the moon, the stars!' It is a modern myth that everyone dislikes being in care.

Rob Brinkworth, Beck's stepson, visits every second Sunday and he took me. When I gave Aunt the roses, she sniffed them and told me to go out into the hall to a cupboard and fetch a vase for them.

She can remember the First World War being declared. (It is like being in the presence of archaeology.) She was eight and in a shed with her father. Her family name was Beck, and being a German name, she said, she knew that when her father and another man spoke of the war, they were worried.

It was Aunt who corrected me when I spoke of Sophia, one of my two granddaughters, as 'the eldest'.

'No, not the eldest,' she said, 'the elder. There are only two.'

I made tea for her, Rob and myself. Cheerful and laughing in a chair, then suddenly moving a stool in front for her feet, she fell backwards with her beautiful legs up—cushions had slipped. She was alright. Rob and I pulled her up and sat her on the foot of the bed. She told us not to tell the nurses, so we did not as she seemed quite recovered. We slunk out waving.

Monday, 27 July

It began to rain again at eight this morning and I started trying to catch up on my diary. It is, though, too cold in the morning to sit in bed writing so it gets neglected.

I'd stop if I could, but because the diary's been going since 1964 it's become a habit, the source of my writing, perhaps. I seem to have a thread in my hands and the days have become a spindle and I dare not abandon the task. What would happen if I did? Nothing much, probably. But I'd feel a traitor to history. A shirker who did not keep the faith. Who would read it? Who would care? Who could untangle the scrawl? It seems perfectly legible, well, not difficult, but most say my writing defeats them, though one friend says the great trick is to read it at speed.

Tuesday, 28 July

My day for Meals on Wheels.

Maria, my driver, has a monologue on her family and takes up the thread where it was left as I leap in and out with the meals while she stays behind the wheel. I do not need to speak—it is like listening to one of Alan Bennett's *Talking Heads* where a person talks in a stream-of-consciousness way, revealing their life more than they know. She is a mild, good woman with a limp; hence staying in the car, listening to Elvis.

'I was thinking about turning the heater on,' an old man says when I remark how cold his house is.

I debate whether to urge him, but hesitate as I know he is worried about the cost. Sometimes I do, sometimes I don't.

Monday, 3 August

Now, in August, seedlings from the fallen tomatoes have risen up and I am watching them, rubbing my hands, in a manner of speaking, thinking that perhaps we will have a crop like that of last summer. But it may be that in such a rich, never cultivated garden there can only ever be one such glorious crop. I walked a barrow load of chicken manure around from my brother's chooks last year and now I need another. Lindy brings me bags of Rooster Booster in her car boot from the garden centre near her. I'll ask for more of that, too. (I can't get it into the panniers on my bike and I don't drive a car.) There may be a limit to what you can ask a brother for because he, too, has a garden.

This brings me to plum trees. I did get a plum tree into a pannier and brought it home safely with the leaves waving in my ears and around my helmet. With what triumph I unloaded it and dug it into the hole near the back door, which faces north. This is a blood plum to fertilise the 'Mariposa' plum which the label says is an improved version of a 'Satsuma'. I had not known that a plum needs another plum of a compatibly fertile type to make fruit. Yet later, Ralph, who is in charge of trees at Bunnings Garden Centre, told me that there is usually a plum within the area that will allow the bees to cross-pollinate your plum.

I heard this after I had bought the blood plum from Ralph and didn't care as I want a lot of plums. In fact, I had four other plums along the side where the tomatoes grew. I didn't know that they are deciduous and that if it is a dry winter, when they are only sticks, they need to be watered. So they never did put on any leaves and had, ruefully, to be dug up. A lesson.

PLUMS AT CLARE

Prunes in the dust
And above, clusters

Like blue testicles,
Rows of plums by the tonne.

I filled the bag
And my mouth.
Their froth cooking
was the colour
of the mousse of the sparkling burgundy
made next door,
which we had for lunch
and the chutney of these plums
enhances cheese
like an old marriage.

Today I went back
and standing inside the tree,
in a nest of plums,
I thought how foreign
this tree is, yet how it thrives here
like our own families,
All of us, plums, people
came here on a boat,
took root
and the plums glowing in jars
stand on the shelf
while the other stalks the land
picking plums, giving thanks
for all red juices.

Friday, 14 August

On some days, the blue flowers starting to blossom on the South African salvia could almost match the sky. But unless I were to lie on the lawn beside the bush and compare it, I cannot be sure, because I learnt from my mother that blue is the hardest colour to match.

When I was about ten years old, she would sometimes send me up to Brocks (Tumby Bay's general store). 'I need you to get me a reel of blue cotton to match the dress I am making you,' she would say. 'Here, take a piece of material.' I would say that I did not need the material as I could tell what shade of blue it was. 'No, you can't, blue is the hardest colour of all to match. You've got to take a cutting with you.'

There were no blue poppies in our lives then although they existed, but there were sometimes Iceland poppies in what were called 'Sunset Shades'. Again I would be sent occasionally after school to Brocks to buy a packet of these seeds. 'Now don't get any other colour,' my mother always said. 'Remember, I want Sunset Shades.'

On the way home I turned the packet over and saw that the colours of the flowers were, in fact, the colours of dawn. I had never seen a sunset because we four children were put to bed at five o'clock. This was because, startling though it now seems, our mother believed that she and our father needed to have their meal on their own and to spend the evening sitting by the fire, if it were winter, listening to the radio while she knitted and sewed.

It was practical in another way as, one by one, the Swiggs' girls, Jane or Mary or Gertie, until they married, would finish their day's work in our house by bathing us and putting us to bed.

Naturally, though we may not have seen a sunset, we always saw the dawn.

Friday, 21 August

A day of croquet minutes, Schubert and Liszt.

As Joanie, my daughter's godmother, and I sat in Elder Hall waiting for Stephen McIntyre to begin playing the piano, she said, 'I've had so much trouble; I spilt coffee over the croquet club minutes and now I'm late and have to decipher them and I am not sure that I can.'

I said, 'Lord, now I know we are old. What are you doing being the secretary when you have only been playing croquet for about a week?'

Ignoring this she said, 'I have got such a sore finger. I've been trying to push safety pins into green ribbons to hold name badges for over a hundred guests at our St Lazarus conference and I see now that it has made the neck ribbons look tatty. So I have to sew the ends of each tiny ribbon together.'

'Why can't you just use safety pins? Nobody would mind.'

'Oh, they would look so shabby over evening gowns and they might get them caught in the fabric.'

I opened the program, realising this was a typical day in her life as a volunteer. Joanie has probably made more sandwiches in four decades than any member of the CWA or Red Cross. Queen of the chicken sandwich. I once asked for her recipe for these and it took two pages to write it down.

Spring

Monday, 14 September

Watching myself age is like watching an explosion far out in a calm sea. So peculiar, so irrationally unexpected. Of course I knew I would age and for some decades I watched the process wryly with a bit of a shrug. But now that real old age has arrived, I see that I did not really expect it at all. It is a paradox. I knew it was coming but I didn't believe it.

An example of this is something so outrageous and vain that it makes me smile when I remember it. For a long time, without realising how old I had visibly become, I would sometimes be surprised when a person would offer to help me lug groceries out of the shop or load them onto my bike, or give me a seat on a bus. I used to think, 'How do they know that I am old?' Truly, I did not think it was visible.

You see, at that time, about four years ago, I felt much the same as I always had. I had the same ardour but not for the same things as I once had. Men were replaced by gardens. The only men I have here now have come to work. It used to be the other way round.

But ardour remained strong and obsessive. So I was blithe about how old I looked.

Friends spoke of needing to take more rest or not being able to do the same things they once did. In fact, it irritated me to be told that I should not do certain work and that I needed to rest.

Once I turned seventy, however, slowly I saw that there had been a change and, say what I would, I had no choice but to take things a bit more easily. Endurance had fled. Stamina and looks, too. Yet I see old people who are beautiful. I wonder at times if they know it. You might ask if I ever thought of looking in the mirror. Well, I did that, noticing ever more wrinkles it is true, but in a perfunctory way which I combined with as much denial as an anorexic about the true state of affairs.

Yet I seize the chance to work because in work lies happiness. Goethe says, 'Whatever you think you can do or believe you can do, begin it. Action has magic, grace and power.'

Thursday, 17 September

Soft rain, off and on all day. Thank heaven. We are desperate for water, but not as desperate as at this time last year. Because of the rain, I sowed seed: a third lot of French bean, because those planted earlier had not sprouted and, of course, I found myself knocking off their new shoots as I dug. Also, a purplish burgundy alyssum called 'Royal Carpet' went into the front garden, along with a flower I have never wanted but now must have. Marigolds. They are to stop nematodes destroying the roots of the new tomatoes which have been planted in places where they grew last summer.

I read that tomatoes should never be planted where they have been in the past year but that, if they are, a crop of mustard seed should be dug in over winter to beat the nematodes. Not having done this and with the tomatoes now planted, I heard at the last minute that marigolds will help.

Cos lettuce seeds went into the seed boxes because yesterday, when going into town to see a film, I craved lettuce. It must have been the hot day.

Down in the western side of the garden, sheltered from the strong sea winds by a high tin fence, a 'Valencia' orange is in full blossom. Having been going on and on about the poor performance of the same type of tree planted at the same time in the front garden, I had not seen the thriving one. A friend pointed this out to me and I was amazed. I never tire of my own whining, but how quickly I tire of it in others.

Today, two local children, Luke and Lauren, were going to garden with me after school but they came and said that it was too wet and that they would return next week. These children with two others had called at the front door about two months ago. I saw shadows on the front window as they walked to the door and, expecting a friend who was taking me to dinner, ran out with my boots in my hands calling 'Welcome! Welcome!'

But it was four children, three from one family. Luke, the eldest, who is eleven, said they were starting their own business and asked if I would like the lawn mowed. I asked if they were fundraising for a charity, but no, it was for themselves. He whipped out a card from his pocket. It read:

Garden Handyman Jobs. Are you tired of having to cut your lawn or trim the old hedge? Don't worry just call up Garden Handy man jobs so you don't have to do it yourself. You pay us what you think is fair. Don't wait ring now. A business run by KIDS. Electricity needed INCLUDES lawn mowing, Hedge trimming. Cleaning up your garden and pruning. Phone number . . . Made by kids for Adults.

Naturally I was entranced. Won over. The lawn was knee-high so I explained that my lawnmower was to be delivered back the next day by the mender, so we need not use their electric one. I said I would pay them $20 and they could work until they thought they had earned that amount.

The next day I heard them before I could see them, trundling down the street with their machine, off to mow a neighbour's lawn. They returned while I was mowing and I gave my machine over to them. Daniel, ten, alarmingly, had a whipper snipper with him which he waved around with elan. I asked if he had his parents' permission to use it and he said he had.

Lauren and Sophie, his younger sisters, ran around with secateurs and a rake, cleaning up with a wheelbarrow for clippings. Sophie's long brown hair blew into her eyes as she ran round and round, waving the secateurs, thin and full of energy. After about an hour, I called them in and gave them hot cocoa and corn muffins at the kitchen bench.

'This is a nice house,' Lauren said.

'Oh, there's more,' I said as I opened the glass sliding door etched with a castle and showed them the living room.

'I like your white couches.'

'We had to take the windows out to get them in.' She hadn't seen plantation shutters before and as all the windows now had them, she was intrigued.

'My mum said you paid $470,000 for this house,' Luke said.

'A bit less than that,' I said, charmed by how natural children can be, saying just what comes to mind. They had some cheese and apples and I handed Luke the money, which he pocketed. Then I gave them a $2 tip each which I would not mention here except that the younger ones quickly handed theirs over to Luke.

'Oh, you're a sort of Mafia Godfather are you?' I said.

'We've made $120 so far.'

'When did you start?'

'Last week.'

I waved them off and said I would call them when I needed more work done.

Walking home from the train yesterday, I ran into Lauren with an eight-year-old girl carrying a baby who, she said, was her sister. I asked if the business was still going and she said that she and Luke were doing it but Daniel had dropped out: that is how those two came to be here today. I tell you, it is like being visited by something wonderful from another place, dolphins, perhaps.

Saturday, 19 September

A wisteria kind of day. It reminds me of the day I sat drinking pisco sours in that seedy hotel bar in Patagonia. Fixated on the cumquat hedge, needing, as I still do, to find more plants to close the gaps, I had forgotten the wisteria until now, because they are blooming and hanging over back fences which I see from the train going in to the city.

Sometimes it seems that the most beautiful plants are those that have been forgotten and just rage on, year after year, because nobody has interfered with them and so they reach their potential. For instance, jasmine, wisteria, convolvulus and old roses sometimes climb quite tall trees if left alone. In another garden I once made, a buttercup-yellow old rose called 'Lady Hillingdon' climbed an olive tree and I didn't see it until it reached the top and bloomed among the grey leaves.

I bought the wisteria at Perry's Fruit and Nut Nursery at McLaren Flat. Joanie and I went to buy a fig to plant by the gate, when there is actually a gate. I saw a patch of wisteria plants growing in a mound of soil and asked if they were for sale. Yes, they were, although the plan was to pot them up because it was late in the season, but the owner pulled on one and it came up with a great coil of root about a metre long. She took it to a shed where a pile of sawdust lay ready to put around bare-rooted trees and there she covered the roots, wrapped it in thick blue plastic and tied it with pink rope.

Now the task is to find something in which to grow this lovely beast because nothing matches wisteria for vigour, weight and ruthlessness. A wisteria can, in time, pull down a verandah, posts and all. At first I thought I'd have a man drill a hole in the cement at the front door, but Lindy said the wisteria roots will grow under the house and will also lift the cement which leads to the door and do the same with the lawn, as it has hers. So a great pot is needed.

Yesterday, drinking tea in a back room at the State Art Gallery, I was staring at two grapevines which grow high on a trellis and saw that they are planted in simple round cement pots about a metre and a half tall. Now where did they get those, and how much did they cost? Not being able to wait to answer these questions nor to afford the pots, I decided to drag in a big terracotta pot of blue petunias which stands in the front garden. I couldn't budge it.

Sunday, 20 September

Soon after dawn, fetching the paper, wearing the old pink dressing-gown, I saw Roland (a young neighbour who mysteriously and daily weeds the immaculate garden of his house, which has stood empty on the corner ever since I have been here). Abandoning shame, I called to him. He came over and together we twisted and turned the pot, waltzing it up to the front step, but could get it no further. He went off to borrow what he called a 'trolley fork' from a friend.

Now to tell you about the great feat of the fig. I was given it at the nursery! A group of tall figs, a metre and a half, stood wrapped in black plastic away from some smaller expensive white figs. I asked the price of the tall ones and was told that they were not self-pollinating and would need a male fig called 'Capri'. Because of this they had not sold well and so I could have one for free. Jubilant, Joanie and I packed it among cushions into the back seat of her car. I thought that I would worry about the problem of pollination later.

Half the night I tossed and turned, wondering if I had been a great fool to think this was a good idea, because now there are three figs in a small garden, so where would 'Capri' go and where would I find one? Then I remembered all the wild figs around, one of which grows in the strip of land among olives and gums beside the nearby train line and has beautiful purple fruit. What pollinates that tree?

I thought also of the enormous old tree in a vacant lot on the way to Glenelg, where I thrice gathered bags and bags of figs last autumn and made chutney. But perhaps these are all self-pollinators? This is all new to me and I see you could go mad thinking of what will pollinate what. It is worse than breeding stud sheep.

FIGS

Figs are old
each tree looks it too
before people spoke
our languages
they ate figs
and no doubt
found them good.

Brown or purple
the skin is queer
striped furry sandpaper
and inside
the rent flesh lies
pink gorgeous wet
it doesn't throb
but it might
and the scent
a mixture
of honey
earth rain
and something green

the white sap
from the stem
turns milk sour
and that you see
is how Adam and Eve
made junket

they used a leaf
as a bowl
and technology was born
can't you see it
rising like Venus
from the cream
stretching its beautiful dangerous arms.

Monday, 21 September

I dug a hole outside near where the gate will be, and put the gift tree in, hoping for a marathon of bees. Surely to heaven there is a male 'Capri' within this figgy sort of suburb.

There is a lot to be said for action. I have never understood how some people could decide to wait a whole year before they plant a garden, because they want to know where the sun falls and what kind of weather they have. You could have something fruiting by then. Perhaps it is just an impetuous nature but then I wonder, how long do those who wait think they are going to live? Yet, when the elderly plant oaks it is a gift to others because they will never see those trees become tall.

Tomorrow, agapanthus.

Thursday, 24 September

A bonanza of cumquats. Lindy and I took a street we don't usually use when we were walking home yesterday because she wanted to show me the bark on some pine trees. After we had seen the thick, tan bark grown into patterns like mud maps of a country, each separate and individual, she showed me an enormous wisteria in bloom. (This was so that I could see how well a wisteria will grow here, the one I bought still bare-rooted in sawdust, waiting for a pot.) It had been woven up a trellis between two posts and was a wall of waving blue.

Beside it was a tree we thought a mandarin. So heavy with fruit the tree was almost entirely coloured orange. As we stood there talking, a woman, hearing us, came out of the house and asked if we would like to come in and pick the cumquats. We would!

We left almost tottering, with the owner, Daphne, waving and telling us to come back for more. Lightning and thunder and then heavy rain. I ran in and out bailing out a bin beneath an overflowing pipe under the gutter, throwing water on every fruit tree in the garden. Unable to go out to buy more sugar, I made nine jars of cumquat marmalade with the sugar which was in the house. The colour is beautiful. This morning, sun was hitting the jars on the bench and I don't know the name of the colour so I must leave you to imagine it. Something like bright, yet darker apricot jam. Amber can be this colour, too.

Last week, I found chervil, which is hard to find, for sale in my second cousin John Brinkworth's nursery, called The Green Room, near here. From him I got a great tall terracotta pot for one third of the price and I am waiting for him to bring it so the wisteria can be planted. And it can't be too soon.

The chervil and basil went into the garden along with a strange and beautiful groundcover called 'Starburst Lotus'. Anything less like a lotus I have not seen. It is a small, grey-blue, slightly succulent-leafed crawling plant with a bright orange flower which points upwards and is shaped a bit like a Sturt's Desert pea. This plant grows in a native garden nearby and we stand, Lindy and I, admiring it, pointing, and wondering what it is. No longer.

If you are not weary of talk of figs, I can say that Mr Perry (who gave me that fig from his orchard, which is now planted where the gate will be one day) said that the fig needs a wasp. It is simply a 'Smyrna' fig and he thinks that, although a male 'Capri' is the correct pollinator, it is possible that any one of those old trees along the railway line here may make it fertile. Or, even perhaps, the 'Brown Turkey' fig in my back garden or the self-sown one I have put outside the western fence to take its chances. This latter, rough old thing has no main stem, but has about seven branches widening out in a circle. I expect it may flourish above all others. I had no idea figs need wasps.

I tried to persuade the nurserywoman to sell me an almond tree. But it was too late in the season and they were being taken up from the earth to be potted and sold in October. I said I would take one bare-rooted but she said there was no certainty it would grow and that it would be better to buy one later when it is in the pot and that it would be the same price. There are thirty-three fruit trees here and although it is a small block, cut in half from what it once was, I am keen for more because I want to grow food, and more food. I think of what will happen if rain becomes less and less. Those with food to share will be popular.

This idea is behind my friend Peri's rare tropical organic orchard in Queensland. She's put four houses on it. She's got four daughters and told me, one day years ago, that if anything like a nuclear war or drought happened, she hoped she'd have a safe place which would feed the girls and their children. It was one of the first illustrations of the way she plans and had a big effect on me. I saw that I had made no such plans and, what's more, had thought that that was normal.

About the same time she said another thing that stayed with me and that was: 'You have to find a way so that when you die, your children can live with themselves over the things they have done to you.'

Sunday, 27 September

Artichokes galore from the hills. Dinah and I have come back from her son Tom's garden at Oakbank. After lunch we went out in gumboots from the shed to the hillside and, in soft rain, cut about five dozen artichokes. There were as many left on the row which went halfway up the hill. On the way, I asked Dinah why Tom had so many artichokes and she said, 'Because he can't do anything small.' I do understand that.

A fortnight ago, Tom sent me about thirty globe artichokes with his mother and, when he heard I had preserved them by boiling them in vinegar and water, draining them, packing them into sterile jars and covering the lot in olive oil, he said we could come up and have as many as I wanted. How many is that? Heaven knows, but it's a lot. We filled the boot of Dinah's car.

Dinah's face was blue from her heart failure when she walked into my kitchen this morning. And it was white as she drove home. I thought as she drove down the winding hills road that it was a far cry from dancing in sequined strapless dresses and thinking that we were the young ones and would always be. (I have just remembered that we were on the same road today when her parents drove us up to her debutante party.)

Today I felt as old as Methuselah. And I understood, as I have for some time, that I would not be young again, which seems blazingly obvious, but it is a surprise, as I said, to find how slow one is to comprehend such a rational thing. For instance, when I serve afternoon tea to the children working in the garden, I feel I am pretending to be an old woman; just going through the motions, as if in a play. I am very convincing.

But the day was glorious. We sat at lunch with Tom's wife, Mandy, a wine-maker, and their three children. We were looking at the dam surrounded by spindly gums with ducks and newly hatched ducklings learning to swim on it. Tom said, 'The ducklings are only a day old and you can still see the shape of the egg on their body. They just have their head sticking up.'

Monday, 28 September

Two of the neighbours' children are in the front garden cutting off the unruly edges of the lawn with spades. Only Luke and Lauren today; the others, it seems, are sick of gardening. They knocked on the back door an hour ago saying that they were ready to work.

Lauren is not strong enough to cut the grass with the spade, even though she stands on it. The lawn just cushions the blade and she wobbles back and forth to no effect. She wanted to mow the lawn and reluctantly I let her for a few minutes while I watched. She assures me her mother says she can mow but Luke says she did not. Compromising, because I didn't want her to feel useless, I let her mow in circles for a while, then took over and gave her a rake so that she could fill the barrow with the lawn cuttings.

They sat on the front bench and had Bickford's lime juice with chocolate biscotti and went back to work. At six, because it was getting dark, Luke asked the time and said dinner would be ready, so they left.

Yellow and orange Iceland poppies are waving at the back door. Spring winds have been stripping off the petals but now, after a day or two of less wind, the petals are back. These poppies and some pots of brown and yellow pansies both came from seed packets which cost a dollar each. There is something satisfying about growing plants from seed. Almost like something from nothing. And it feels frugal, too.

The wisteria I bought bare-rooted on the same day as I was given the fig was planted last week in a big pot at the front door. My second cousin John delivered the pot and gave me much good advice.

First of all, looking at the cumquat hedge, many of which plants he had sold me, now so battered and shredded, he said, 'Citrus hate wind.' I said I had recently been told that and I couldn't yet afford a fence.

Then he said, 'Well, if I were you, I'd take off all the fruit and flowers. Then I'd cut back any bits of dead wood because the tree will still be trying to pump energy into those bits. When there is a lemon like that at the nursery, I take it away and shelter it, feed it and give it a chance. But often, they don't really come back properly.'

After he left I took the secateurs and did as he said. Tearing off hundreds of green cumquats felt perverse, and now there is a ring of fruit around the trunk of each tree and I am wiser.

The apricot and the plum trees, though! Hundreds of tiny, hard green fruit on both and it happened within, it seems, about a day or three of the petals falling.

Wednesday, 30 September

Naked ladies: *Amaryllis belladonna*. I was passing my brother Peter's neighbour's garden which was being dug up, cement and all, by a man with a small bulldozer. Seeing a pile of what looked like agapanthus, I asked the man if he was planning to replant them. He said he was not the owner, who was in the house. I knocked on the door and was told that indeed he had just dug them up himself that morning and would use them, but he said I could take two. I walked over to the heap and picked up a single clump of the strappy leaves which proved to have four large white bulbs stuck together on the end. I dropped them into the pannier on my bike and rode home, wondering what they could be. It looked like a lily bulb.

On Monday Luke and I separated the bulbs and he laid them out in a row to see how we could make a rhythm of plants along the outside of the western fence. Then he dug four holes where I had put white and blue agapanthus last week and together we planted the bulbs. I tipped on them the water in which they had rested in the barrow.

Still puzzled about what the plant really was, I came inside and rang my friend Laurel at Peel. She said they are probably naked ladies which are usually pink and sometimes white. I love an eccentric line. Talk about Kandinsky. Now there will be a small hedge of pink, white and blue at the base of that green fence. I had said to Luke as he dug, and Lauren swept, 'Now you will be able to see these plants when you walk to school and you will remember that you planted them.'

I thought of the saying, 'When Adam delved and Eve span, who was then the gentleman?'

I asked Luke if he had a garden and he said he has and that he will be growing his own food when he grows up.

A man after my own heart. I told him he could have some 'Grosse Lisse' tomato seedlings next time he comes here.

Friday, 2 October

Never plant alstroemeria unless they are of a kind that will not multiply to become a weed. I have been around at my friend Jane's house weeding out alstroemerias. There is no poison which she can discover that will kill them. A couple of years ago her gardener actually sieved the whole garden to be rid of them. But they are back as bad as ever and, like onion weed, each has hundreds of tiny bulbs which, even if you sieve over the ground, will just rise again.

Covering them all in thick wads of newspaper and putting mulch on top will not eradicate them. I got rid of onion weed with this method in my last garden yet it took about three years. But these flowers are not in swathes, they are among everything—down the side garden, around the grapevine, under the hellebores, the lemon, the persimmon, and everything else; there is no place where they do not thrive.

Spring

Jane is one of the nurses and later we went to university together. She says of herself she has a mind like a rat trap. She can remember every published detail of the Peloponnesian Wars and I can only remember Pericles.

Fate has seen to it that Jane must simply watch these weeds go on invading. She has a neck like a piece of coral and can rarely bend to weed. It reminds me of the Countess Elizabeth, the author of that early bestseller of nature writing called *Elizabeth and Her German Garden* who, because of her status, was not allowed to dig, weed, plant or prune. She could only gather flowers while the gardeners did the work. It drove her half mad.

Here, sweet peas are in full bloom. I have rigged up a set of wire coathangers on chicken netting and old poles to make a fence for them. In the street six weeks ago, I found a set of wire shelves which I brought home and leant among the wires so that the sweet peas could cling to them. And now they do. Everybody loves them for their scent and yet some have been bred with less and less scent. Those in bunches sold at fruit and flower carts in Rundle Mall have no scent at all.

Tuesday, 6 October

Iris galore. This abundance of flowers with nothing but sun and rain shows what we can do if we look around old towns. They must have got away from a farmhouse. I feel greedy and amazed when I look at the bounty.

It was Sunday and wild white iris were blooming in clumps along the roadside and in paddocks around Auburn when my brother Bill and his wife Pamela drove me home to their stables at Stockport. Thousands and thousands of iris. He didn't want to stop, but he did.

Pamela and I walked across the road and Bill got out a hammer and a box from the car. Having no spade, as they had just cleaned out Pamela's car from a trip across the Simpson Desert, Bill used the hammer to dig up the iris rhizomes. Pamela said, 'I use this hammer to break stones.' A puzzling thing. I asked what she meant. 'Oh, I use it when I need to break stones to dig a hole for a fire for the camp oven.' A very Australian answer, I thought.

We pulled into their driveway and Pamela showed me where she'd like the iris planted in the front garden. She dragged a long hose over and began to water the native shrubs, while I planted. Because Bill and Pamela can be away for up to thirty-three days at a time, taking people over deserts, everything needs to be either succulents in pots on the 70 metres of verandah or a native or an agapanthus.

Earlier, we had been to Auburn market and there was an iris stall where they cost $6 each. So these free iris seemed manna from heaven. I packed some of the iris to take home, so much for sticking to the orange and blue. But when a thing is free and beautiful and needs no extra water, I give in.

And white is not a colour.

I have since looked up *Botanica* and think that these are *Iris germanica*. We used to call them flags. The big petals flop and droop like a flag.

After a couple of hours we came in and sat around the fire with a drink while we talked about what else we could do in the garden. A couple of grapevines would shade the back verandah. And bougainvillea and a wisteria along the front. Odd how addictive and consuming a garden can be, even someone else's. It can take over a night and be the subject of dreams and a lot of tossing around, tormenting your sleep.

Wednesday, 7 October

Marigold plants went in beside tomatoes and a punnet of mixed lettuce, too. Dull things, but necessary.

The quince tree has four green rosebuds of leaves ready to burst and the wisteria in the new pot has lifted up and looks well. They are tough things, I am told, and have a root run of more than 20 metres. I saw a wisteria bring down half a verandah when I stayed at a restaurant, closed at the time, called Skillogolee at Clare. It's since been mended, that verandah, but it was a glorious sight; a shredded curtain of blue flowers drooping like a sad lost love. I lay in bed with Mr Wrong and felt I could hardly breathe. What it proved to be was not the sight of the wisteria, but asthma. The doctor said that a mould grows on grapes in late autumn and it sets asthmatics off.

And now, remembering all this, I have exploded a carton of frozen cream in the microwave.

Saturday, 10 October

A revelation. This morning, lying in bed listening to a radio garden show, some advice was given that explained how I killed two lemon trees. The gardener said that a new lemon tree must have all the potting mix removed from its roots by dipping it into a bucket of water and easing off every scrap. If this is not done, the roots don't get a proper chance to break out of their pot's mould and reach into the new soil. They grow in a stunted fashion, if at all, and the roots remain coiled.

This is contrary to everything I have been doing which was to drop the tree into the hole gently, keeping as much of the mix around the roots as possible. This probably explains why the eighteen cumquats, the oranges and the mandarin are not thriving. Wind has not helped, but a healthy tree can bear wind.

LEMON

Bitter breast
of the earth
I've picked this one
from a dark green laden tree

This is a cold hard
obdurate fruit
yet one swift act
releases the juice
enhancing oysters
fish and almost everything else

the acerbic aunt
of the orchard
beautiful in youth
yet growing thorny
in old age
irritating
irritable

Spring

when I move house
the first tree I plant
is a lemon

biblical
dour and versatile
I much prefer it
to those cloying salesgirls
the soft stone fruits.

That gardener on the radio said that this method of planting lemon trees has been used in the horticultural industry for twenty, maybe thirty years. If so, why was it such news to me? Surely I can't be the only one who didn't know of it. Now I am tempted to dig up some of the other citrus, but with six days of more than 35-degree heat forecast, it is not the right time.

After hearing this revolutionary method of planting citrus trees, I lay on my bed, brooding over this. A curious sight appeared. Sparrows, which only days before had been mating on the Stobie pole directly in my line of vision from the pillows, were darting in and out of the hollow top cross-beam of the pole. They must be feeding their young. Every two minutes or so, a sparrow would fly up from one of the wires below, pause on a wire near the entrance and enter. A moment later it emerged. In between times a pair mated thrice, in their usual quick way.

Now I have, in my day, been a busy young mother of two with a business on the premises, so I was impressed. Having no way of distinguishing the birds (and there were four or five of them) I cannot say which sparrows mated and which entered the hollow. They must have been feeding young, because if eggs were hatching there would not have been this continual flying in and out.

Then the thought occurred to me: 'If it is 35 degrees today, how can fledglings live in this narrow hollow beam of what surely must be steel, for the next hot week?' There is not a shred of protection from the sun which was beating down as I watched. This thought was so disturbing it forced me to rise and dig up the mandarin tree which stands between Nora's house and mine in an effort to exert some power over nature, trivial though it was.

Nora had greeted me when I first introduced myself with the words, 'When are you going to get rid of the strelitzia?'

'Well, I wasn't planning to.'

'My son says he'll burn it down.' (Welcome to Hove.)

'Nora, it would take a backhoe to get that plant out.'

She said, 'It sticks into my letterbox.'

I said, 'Oh, I can fix that,' and I ran and got secateurs and pruned the leaves and stems on her side.

Now the mandarin has been there for eighteen months and no matter how much blood and bone, chicken manure and water it has been given, it has not thrived. I plunged it into a big bucket of water and saw that the roots are coiled into a corkscrew shape like a bonsai tree. The poor plant had no chance to take in nourishment, because it was choked with its original potting mix. I tore off all the mix and hosed the roots thoroughly. There was one longish root which was able to be freed so now it lies stretched out away from the trunk and the tree will either die or thrive.

Tuesday, 13 October

Tuesday is my Meals on Wheels day. Into each house on our list I fly with the meal and merry cries. We are not encouraged to linger, although it is my profound instinct to stay and talk. Conversation seems almost as important as food in some cases.

For instance, once one old man, to whom we'd been delivering meals for months, said his wife was coming home from hospital that afternoon. A breathtakingly thin type of wolfhound lay on the floor, dying, perhaps. It was winter and the room was cold.

I said, 'It's cold in here for your dog.'

He said, 'Oh well, turn the air-conditioning on, will you? It's that switch on the wall.'

From then on, through the next summer, I mentioned the dog in the heat as he sat there sweltering. Each time he told me to turn the air-conditioning on. His wife died during this time and he sat, day after day, an effigy of sadness with the dog growing thinner.

'There's a strong smell in here. What is it?'

'Oh, the dog's been sick. I've cleaned it up with the dustpan.'

'Can I help?'

'My wife's got a cupboard of stuff in the passage. You can use some of that.'

I took the Pine O Cleen and a rag and did my best.

Soon after this, no dog. 'What's happened to your dog?' I asked.

'The vet put him down. There was no need. He was alright. My daughter took the dog to the vet in her station wagon and when she opened the back, he tried to jump out but he fell on the road. The vet saw it and put him down. There was no need.'

Faced with this double grief, I pointed to the mass of white tulips in the front.

'They're my wife's.'

Wednesday, 14 October

Amazing how engaging a Stobie pole can become. (The Stobie pole was invented by the father of an ophthalmologist I worked for before I was married. Shortage of timber to hold powerlines and street lights meant that his invention of using concrete poured between sections of railway line, left then to set and raised as a pole, filled the need.)

All yesterday afternoon, even at the hottest time of the day when it reached 38 degrees, those sparrows flew in and out of the hollow beam. Then I saw that the same thing was happening at the other end. The heat beat down, yet the chicks inside must have survived because soon after dawn the flights began. These frantic flights of feeding remind me of the Berlin airlift when the Allies broke the Soviet blockade by flying hundreds of thousands of tonnes of food to West Berlin.

It will be clear by now that there is a great deal of time being spent, head on pillow, watching these sparrows. This pole, I see now, is their tree and it may be that with the hollow for nests inside the beams, it is safer than open nests in a real tree. But in a tree, they'd have a sweet wind to cool the nestlings from time to time.

I am besotted with watching these birds and it now occurs to me, in a superstitious way, that if the fledglings survive and if—oh! miracle—I were to see one fly down from the nest, all would be well and the healing we so badly need would happen. Odd, when you have no power, how superstition rises like a wraith, mad and inexplicable. Call it faith, and it will feel a bit better. But faith asks for nothing to happen; it just is . . .

FAITH

Life is a fox slinking
beside the stone fence
its tail throbbing along
like a red feather above the stormy sea.
Jack, twenty-three, longs to see
a wolf in January.
I like the blue horse which comprises
salvia, lavender and Russian sage
its mane waving outside this window
Tibetan prayer flags flutter
above the verandah opposite
my son's house and his daughter's hair
loose or in ponytails are the flags
we love. They make us jubilant
and grateful, amazed at the other miracle
this wind of hope. This morning I read
that Duchess pears are self-pollinating
but Mariposa plums are not. I saw that
faith's a pollinator too, if I can live
with doubt. It's like breathing in and out.
In is faith, out is doubt. Both comprise
the whole and bear sweet fruit.

Thursday, 15 October

An unusually cold October. Sharp wind hits me when I ride to the shops and yet, sheltered in the back garden, there is warmth. The two grapevines there are shooting up the fence behind the Christmas lilies which have multiplied, even, I think, doubled. Jane said that these bulbs now have to be used as an annual because the heat of these recent summers kills them after they have flowered. Yet these bulbs are thriving from last summer and it is, I suppose, because they live in the shade of a small fig and the back fence.

While I never argue with climate change sceptics, neither do I entirely believe we are doomed. If the weather is heating up, why this cold October? People hold strong views on these matters and are easily annoyed by any mere comment, so I hold my tongue, as a sister would. There is a children's fable where, my old friend Peri tells me, a sister has to save her seven brothers by knitting them a nettle jacket each. As she has four brothers and I three, we nodded at each other knowingly. Having an argument is not going to change the weather, anyway. The glaciers go on melting.

I have been out potting up cuttings to take to Bill and Pamela. Spurge (*Euphorbia* species), daisies, rosemary, plumbago, lavender, pelargoniums and geraniums. These old plants are tough, like the old boxers you see at bars in pubs late in the morning. Can't be killed with alcohol or blows. Yet frost can kill geraniums, I recall.

As I pass the garden where I was given the bulbs of naked ladies, I see the remainder lying baking in the sun. They are leached of green already. It is tempting to creep in and throw a bucket of water over them and toss over a tarpaulin which lies beside them. But sometimes people do not like interference, even if it is helpful.

I've had a few shocks about that lately so am being careful.

'In the end, we all marry ourselves,' Rudolf Nureyev said. I think he's right. All day I discuss things with myself; argue, telling myself off, say that I am a fool. Impatient, accepting, resigned, it is a marriage of a sort. Then there is the idea of the garden and I am married to that, too. Marrying a garden is more like young love. Seething with plans, full of hope. Willing to brook no opposition. Visions, visions. You don't think of bushfire, flood, calamity. You go to it with open arms, and a spade, perhaps, under your elbow.

I see the tenderness of old married men who come out to greet me when I bring their Meals on Wheels. They come with trays on pushers, nod, say their thanks, take the meals onto the tray and turn back; pushing it indoors to their waiting wife. I see the chaos of the abandoned garden, which they either see and despair of, or have never, perhaps, cared about. Weeds waving around the letterbox. A desert of lawn and a dying central tree. All this is beyond nagging: we are now down to central things. Kindness, patience, tenderness, resignation and a few last pleasures. Wine and books in some cases. Football on TV, whatever takes their fancy. Less pain is what I wish for them and to enjoy the meal.

I come home to my own marriage to myself exhilarated with gratitude.

Friday, 16 October

A day of clouds and lettuces. As the train went into town, I read an *Organic Gardener* magazine describing how to germinate lettuce and how to grow them. I looked at the sky and saw clouds the shape of feathers, and the feathers made the shape of a peach. (I stared and stared and wished, for once in my life, and it is about the only time, that I had a camera.) Why was it not an apple? I can't say, but it looked like a peach to me. When the clouds were past, I went back to the lettuces.

Having planted lettuces two days ago, I read that you should choose small fresh plants and half an hour before planting, soak them in a bucket of water laced with liquid seaweed mixture or worm castings, or compost tea made from compost soaked in water.

But it was the seed advice that was puzzling. Having read somewhere that the seeds won't germinate unless they are placed in a temperature of less than 25 degrees, it seemed that placing them on a sheet of kitchen paper and putting them in the fridge for a day or so would do the trick. Now I read that the seeds need light. No fridge has light when closed, as far as I know.

Burying the seed too deeply prevents germination. They are supposed to be sprinkled on the soil and just watered in so that the seed falls into the cracks. One pinch of seed per person in the household. Day after day I have peered at the seed box waiting for the cos lettuces to sprout. Something has, and maybe it is lettuce, perhaps marigolds. It doesn't matter much, either or both would be welcome. These are sweet conundrums, trivial, but they make my life seem meaningful.

Saturday, 17 October

Sometimes, when bent over weeding, my mind wanders to other things. I wondered recently about ageing women's sexuality and my own in particular.

In Jane Miller's book on ageing, *Crazy Age: Thoughts on Being*

Old (Virago, 2010), she says that she is glad to be past feeling sexual and is now happy rushing off to swim daily in the local indoor pool; it has come as 'a relief, but also a surprise'.

Never trust a married woman writing about her sexuality if she is denying it. Perhaps it is hard to know if you are being honest when you know your husband will read what you have written and it must be especially difficult when you know that the magazine he began, the *London Review of Books*, is likely to review your book.

In marriages I have watched or read of, both are able to agree, silently or not, that they are over it, and that they can live happily together sharing much else. They have no need to grieve for the loss; they can throw themselves into work, sport, gardening, music, the family and other pleasures. However, take one of them out of the equation and, my Lord, a phoenix can rise to the astonishment of the owner and perhaps to others, too.

Much depends on pheromones. Even working with somebody of the sex you find attractive can have an effect. A sudden clenching of the stomach that must be hidden. A deep breath, and their smell can have a stirring effect.

No, the married woman cannot be relied on unless she has had a wide experience.

However, a single old woman might be a bit more reliable. But not with any certainty. For instance, I was at the Town Hall recently listening to a cello concerto when I began wondering what had happened to my sexuality. These thoughts rise more often in me during opera, but they come watching and listening to classical music, too. I don't know if this happens to others.

Suddenly while the cellist played I thought, 'Where has my sexuality gone?'

And the answer came. 'It has gone like a wild horse into the forest.'

Then, 'It is grazing quietly and may never return.'

There was a pause and I heard the cellist. The thought came, 'Yet it might; it has in the past.'

I threw the last weeds onto the lawn to mow later and went inside. Contemplating the question. Now I ask myself, 'Do I want it (my sexuality) to return?'

So far no. The price is too high.

I remember once walking home through the parklands, stopping to look at a tree and so filled with sexual longing I wanted to love that tree. (No, not make love to the tree, but to turn the feeling into love.) I wanted to be able to take that feeling from me and throw it into a lake or turn it into a tree, perhaps. It may be that is where my passion for tree planting has come from.

That's a new thought.

Yet there is a certain man who surprises me sometimes, and this is now very rare—after we leave a restaurant, as we pass under a shady tree, away from common view, he presses me to his chest kisses me, releases me and together we walk the path side by side. If we were to go to his hotel, there would be no end of it and I do not want to suffer that. So this is a better thing. The horse has put its beautiful, noble head out from the foliage of the forest for a moment and disappeared back into the darkness.

Tuesday, 20 October

For two days the wind has blown, and all night, too. Gale warnings galore. I have been out and dressed the blood orange tree down the side in a sarong, sheltered though it is by the western fence. Half the leaves have gone so I propped an old towel up on the garden fork and a window screen before growing more desperate, going indoors and finding the sarong. The tree looks as if it has come in from the beach. Behind this citrus, I sowed a dozen soaked sunflower seeds.

My niece, Annabel, Tucker's daughter, says that chooks are in our destiny. Because of this, she sent these seeds so that when I get poultry, I will be able to feed them one sunflower head a week. She is out scouring the suburbs for hard rubbish to make a chook shed for herself and for me. I have gone along with all this, as it may be just play, although I don't know where the chooks could be penned here. There is only cement outside the kitchen window, which would be where the shed could go. Sometimes things just evolve. If I can find a man with a jackhammer who doesn't charge, I could have the cement dug up. Then the chooks could scratch the ground and I would get manure as well as eggs, perhaps.

Yesterday in the early dusk, I took packets of seed out to the front garden and sowed directly into the earth 'Roma' tomatoes, capsicum, eggplant and cucumber. None of those I sowed there earlier in spring have come up. I think it must be that ants take them. There were ants running up my leg and one on my back when I weeded before planting about fifty orange cosmos seedlings from the seed box. Last summer these cosmos waved above all else as I lay in bed and watched them. I cannot tell you what a cheerful sight that was on waking.

Wednesday, 21 October

Day after day I search for the morning star. Last winter it set above the Stobie pole while two planes flew over towards the airport in the north-east. Now, a gum tree across the road, which was a sapling then, has grown wide and tall and even if the star were there, the gum will soon obscure it. Where this star has gone, I do not know. It gave me pleasure to watch it when I woke. Clouds can't always shield it.

Lindy brought me a pink envelope of seeds of snow-on-the-mountain today. Months ago, when we walked in a street which was unknown to us, we saw a marvellous green and white plant in a new cottage garden. Lindy knocked on the door and a woman answered and, hearing Lindy's name, said that years ago she had known her parents and their vineyard and winery, St Hallett, at Tanunda. She told us the name of the plant and said that she would save seed for us. This is not a plant or, as far as we can tell, a seed that you can buy from a nursery.

I sowed these seeds in the seed box that had been emptied of cosmos, came indoors and, thinking I would not be likely to find the botanical name, found it almost at once. It is *Euphorbia marginata*, also called ghostweed. It is fairly fast growing to 60 centimetres with a spread of about half of that. It endures cold. Let us hope it will endure heat. But it must, or it would not have survived here with those fifteen days of over 35 degrees last summer. Now I read in *Botanica* that there are more than 2000 species of euphorbia, among them annuals, herbaceous perennials, shrubs and succulents which at first sight look like cacti.

Mint is choking the thyme so from time to time I pull some out and plant it in the front lawn so that when it is mowed it will give out its perfume. Odd ideas like this may be silly and come to nothing, even making a nuisance of the mint, but I could be glad.

There is a word for a plant which releases its perfume when you brush against it. I knew that word once and now cannot look it up, because to look up a word, you need to know it. (Unless you use a thesaurus and even then you need to have something to hang the investigation on.) And no one I ask can tell me what it is. These plants, such as lavender, rosemary and scented geraniums, are put beside doorways, steps and entrances and there is a general word which describes them, but it has vanished.

At a doctor's surgery, I read a pamphlet on Alzheimer's disease which said that when you forget a word, it is not indicative of that disease if you remember it later. If it vanishes forever, though, it can be one of the symptoms. The word I forget and then remember hours or days later is fibroid. And for Lindy, the forgotten word is the name of a plant, cyclamen. There is another plant the name of which I have trouble with: I can only say that it is a tall, grey-leafed, hardy shrub with great spikes covered in blue flowers. The spikes are not unlike the enormous agave flower here, which, day after day, bends lower as if the Sydney Harbour Bridge were slowly sinking into the sea.

Last weekend, I cut ten big agaves with a Japanese saw and left them in a wheelbarrow and on the ground for my brother Bill to collect while I was out. They were for his daughter Stephanie's new garden at Gawler.

Monday, 26 October

Lord, the wind. It seems to have doubled. I went out to check on the blood orange tree, and found that the sarong had risen up and, as if it were a shy child, I pulled the skirt down over the trunk, readjusted the towel and left it to its suffering.

Wednesday, 4 November

Still the wind blows. However, the gale warnings have changed to those of strong wind. How the lambing is going, I don't know. I think that if it is hard for orange trees, what must it be like for animals giving birth in these winds? The way animals simply hang their heads and suffer. I love to think of my brother Tucker keeping mallee scrub trees on low hilltops where deer, sheep and cattle can shelter. By keeping trees, I mean not removing them to make pasture. This, of course, also helps maintain the water table and keeps salt at bay, but that's another story and a long one.

On quite another matter, two nights ago, I took the cos lettuce seeds from the fridge and laid them out on a dish, still on the wet kitchen paper on which they were sown. I left them in the light of the kitchen, hoping to combine those two conflicting pieces of information, cold and light, which they need to germinate. Lo and behold! Next morning, when I took them out to the seed box, they had grown white tails, like tadpoles. I felt as if I had discovered penicillin. I keep saying to myself over and over 'I have activated the endosperm.'

Some of these seeds I brushed gently off into the soil: the rest I left where they were and laid the paper down on the seed box with the seeds facing the soil, leaving the paper above, watered it and now it's wait to see. And if, by the end of this book, there is caesar salad being made, you will be the first to know.

Friday, 6 November

Today beside this street's signpost, I transplanted a brugmansia, which has an apricot flower. Lindy had struck this from two cuttings

I gave her from a young tree on Peri's farm in Queensland. While my two cuttings sit in the front garden, still green, but with no leaves, this one has spurred ahead and is a foot tall with many leaves. I think it should look wonderful draping the sign which vandals keep trying, for some mad reason, to push over. It seems that to be a vandal, one must be in a considerable state of fury, similar to a hard case of PMT.

Saturday, 7 November

The wind has dropped. Outside the kitchen window, Nora's pomegranate tree stands before an enormous grapefruit tree which is covered in yellow fruit. Neither of these trees, as far as I know, have a jot of food, pruning or water and yet they show what this climate and soil can do. Beyond these, in someone else's garden behind a tall galvanised iron fence, a lemon tree about 4 metres high is also laden. I see now that it must be the nursing of trees in their first years that is important. Once they are big enough they seem to be able to shield themselves from wind and even heat.

Late one afternoon this week, I took the bucket of dahlia roots out to the front garden and, crouching out of the wind, dug them in around the small tormented orange. (The blood orange in the side garden is still draped in its sarong.) The dahlias may make a shelter for the tree in the summer or, if not, I can take it to Stephanie at Gawler since she has shelter and the tree may thrive.

I am sick of trying to shelter trees. Thirty-three of them and none need anything more than what they have abundantly—mulch, fertiliser, buckets of water—except the thing they most need, shelter, which I can't give.

The dahlias were beautiful last autumn, bright orange, like stars. I dug them up in winter and need to remember next time to use a fork because a spade can cut the tuber, just as it does with potatoes.

Speaking of potatoes, those who have tasted a newly dug dish of potatoes know what a surprise freshness makes to this, the most reliable of vegetables. Fresh, it is almost a different food. My brother Peter said he had been around recently when I was out and dug up a few kilos for himself because he had run out and the shops were shut. I can tell you there was pleasure in hearing this. Pleasure at the trust and pride, too, that I could give him something.

Sparrows are drinking and washing in the water bowl on the gravel in the back garden where the great new shed once was, right up against the house. I told the owner I would have the shed taken away and he asked why. I said that I have nothing to put in it except the bike. So it came down in the first month and it cost nothing because Scott, who did the work, built another shed with the materials and sold it.

Is there anything more calming than to watch birds drink and wash in a bowl? Day after day after lunch I lie in the back room and watch the birds. The Murray magpie stalks around the garden like a prospective buyer sticking its beak into everything then, finding nothing to please it, flies up to the fence, pauses and goes off.

Then comes the black scratcher. At the foot of the apricot among the new basil, and around the two grapevines, the lilies and the plum, it goes berserk. Dirt flies up. It must be searching for insects. Although I prefer an untidy garden to a neat one, this bird is hard to bear. I never knew it before I came here. It is like someone destroying her house in a strange spasm. And, what's more, doing it again and again, day after day. It's almost hypnotic to watch, and possibly the bird itself is hypnotised by its work.

Then there are the parrots. The glorious parrots. They flit down onto the front lawn of dandelions and I look out through the shutters in my bedroom and say, 'Oh, hello!' Yesterday, one with a red head and breast, and acid yellow-green body with blue and black tail feathers, strutted around in an elderly fashion, nibbling at the flowers as if at a bowl of nuts on a bar. Three or four green and crimson rosellas fly down from the tall gums which are in blossom, stroll around a while and fly up. Once or twice passing these trees on my bike, a rosella has flown down so fast that, not hearing or seeing me, it has had to dodge the bike, this vehicle like an iron hawk.

Sunday, 8 November

Entangled in one of life's more brilliant snares, which do not concern us here, the garden is a miracle of consolation. Even such a little thing as transplanting beetroot sown in the seed box months ago, along with spinach and some unknown thing which may be tomatoes so young that I can't tell, is almost mystical the way it soothes me.

We have had days of brilliant sunny weather. Iron chelates are my new thing for the thirty citrus trees. Paula, my friend from Mornington in Victoria, who has been staying with me, took a yellowing leaf of a cumquat in her hand and said, 'This tree needs chelates.' Odd how, having read for months about the use of iron chelates for citrus and potassium for tomatoes, I have ignored this advice because these tonics are expensive and yet, on hearing Paula speak of it, I could barely wait to buy them. I used to think that I would just use hefty doses of blood and bone and chicken manure and all would be well. Not so.

Paula is one of the nurses. When she married her late husband, she went to live in Mornington. I never knew anyone who hated cold weather so much and loved the sun. There's a lot of the former where she went to live. For shining integrity, she has no peer.

Later, Peter, told as I sat at his table that I was on my way to buy chelates, walked to the shed and returned with a box which he put in my hand. I rode home and made a right royal turmeric yellow mix in a bucket and gave all the trees half a bucketful each. Even the figs and plums and the apricot got a dose.

Paula and her partner, David, and I went to a nursery at McLaren Vale and I bought the last of their agapanthus, thrown into a box among the soil in which they had grown. They were selling capers, too, so I bought a bush and a punnet of eggplant seedlings. Then I saw they had 'Thompson Seedless' grapevines in pots, which I had been searching for, so I bought two of them. David planted one at the back of the house into a hole dug in the cement where the shed once stood. It will shade the house along with the two glory vines which I had planted when I first came. I wish now I had used all fruiting grapes but I had known that they bring bees and that could be a problem.

'The day will come, my girl, when you will want for fruit!' was what Granny Shemmald said to my mother when she threw quinces at her sister Nora. It echoed in my mother's mind because when she was first married and went to Tumby Bay there was no fruit other than the native quandong. The only other fruit came by sea on the ship *Moonta*.

THE AUNTS

All my aunts are dying.
Their bones in the tissue paper parcels
of their hands
pleat the past into the edges of the sheets.

They don't flirt now
or pelt each other with fruit
or toss their heads
at cheeky boys.

Their red hair or black
is grey now
'Straight as a yard of pump water'
as Granny used to say
permanently curled on their pillows
they lie
gesturing vaguely
at their future
which is as clear
as the water in the glass jug.

I have never understood why no fruit trees were planted at Tumby Bay or, if they were, we did not know of them. People had water tanks and sometimes wells or underground tanks which held water collected from the roof. Bathwater and washing-up water from a tin basin went onto the tomatoes, but not onto fruit trees.

Now, every tree and vine in this garden ought, I feel, to feed people. Famine may be coming. Why do I feel this? I don't know, but the newspapers give gloomy reports on weather and population. Perhaps it is just some atavistic impulse, deeply ingrained. All those German ancestors who piled their cellars full for winter and waited it out, prepared as ants.

My own cupboards are nothing to sniff at, with pickled eggplant, artichokes, lemon and mustard pickle, green tomato chutney, red tomato chutney, cumquat marmalade, more than I could use, preserved quinces and figs, and the rest is wine. And, if that seems a lot for a single woman, Peter has walls of jam. Yes, hundreds of jars. All exquisite food: he has so much, he sells it.

These impulses go deep in our family and must be genetic. Yet my Scottish grandmother never pickled or preserved a thing in her life, as far as I know. In fact, when grandfather went to war at Gallipoli, she took their two sons and moved into a boarding house. Perfect! At last, no cooking!

Monday, 9 November

Soon after dawn, when I raise the blind, sparrows are mating on the Stobie pole outside the garden. Thrice, or more it goes on, the male flies up to a higher wire then drops down onto the hen. It seems a sign of optimism and fertility, and if I push the idea it can augur a good day. Amazingly, ten times it went on with one pair until the hen flew away. I found a pale blue egg a month ago and showed it to the two children who had been gardening and were sitting on the garden bench outside my room, drinking lime juice. When I went back it was broken, dropped. But at least they saw and held it.

The small blackbirds which scratch the earth are in a frenzy lately. No matter what is laid down on the beds to deter them— garden tools, poles, rope, an old umbrella, fly screens, buckets, half-dead strelitzia flowers and leaves thrown out from vases—these birds persevere. Lettuce and coriander have gone, and basil, too. Today I saw an advertisement for a singing rope which, it is said, will deter cats and birds. The rope, I think, must hum and let out a high noise heard only by dogs and cats and birds. But I'd rather buy some potash for the tomatoes. Every now and then I rush through the back door, shouting to scare the birds away from the lettuce. Is it worth it? Probably not.

In an anthology Charles Dudley Warner wrote a piece on insects called 'My Summer in a Garden', published by the Royal Horticultural Society in 1871, which reminded me of this daft bird and its torment:

I awake in the morning and a thriving garden will wake a person two hours before he ought to be out of bed and think of the tomato plants—the leaves like fine lace-work, owing to black bugs that skip around, and can't be caught. Somebody ought to get up before the dew is off (why don't the dew stay on till after a reasonable breakfast?) and sprinkle soot on the leaves. I wonder if it is I. Soot is so much blacker than the bugs that they are disgusted, and go away. You can't get up too early, if you have a garden. You must be early due yourself, if you get ahead of the bugs. I think that, on the whole, it would be best to sit up all night, and sleep daytimes. Things appear to go on in the night in the garden uncommonly. It would be less trouble to stay up than it is to get up so early.

It has the utterly fed-up, exasperated tone that I like.

Reading these dead gardeners I feel as if we are having a conversation, the dead and the living, as warm and interesting as if both were alive and one was peering over the other's gate.

I used to love nightclubs, now I love nurseries.

Wednesday, 11 November

A warm day, 29 degrees and 36 forecast for Sunday. By January, if this keeps up, this garden will need shadecloth. It felt like fumigating a hospital today when I came home with a form of sterilising chemical and threw it all around the garden. Tomato dust galore on the tomatoes, hoping no bees were near their flowers. Then potash at the base of the tomatoes and sterile seed-raising soil into the seed boxes. Dusting off my hands like Matron after inspecting the wards, I came indoors and cleaned the oven.

I can do nothing for the caper bush I trod on. I haven't touched the small broken branches and have just kept it moist, thinking it may be best to let it heal itself, if indeed it can. A plum tree Lindy gave me, speaking of forms of recovery, now has three green branches from the root stock, even though the grafted trunk is dead. I took a saw out at dusk and cut off the dead trunk and noticed even more greenery growing from the base. It will not matter what plum this turns out to be.

There is now a glut of spinach and 'Sugarloaf' cabbages and I see, with surprise, how wasteful this has made me. I tip into the compost what, a week ago, I would have kept and even gloated over. Foxgloves, which I hardly like to mention, having not meant to have a romantic garden, have been surprising with their big stems covered in flowers, and then more and more rising from around the main stem. You can plan all you like but one moment of weakness at the nursery and the plan is broken.

Sometimes it seems that the people who stick to their plans are landscape architects and it is in another person's garden that the sternness is applied. Years of experience possibly helps to avoid these lapses of foxgloves. But I still haven't got a rose, so all is not lost.

One of the great gardens of Chile, the Rencorets' garden in Santiago, was designed by Juan Grimm. He would have no truck with roses but Mrs Rencoret wanted them. This was, I think, early on in his career: he is much stricter now. One day, as these two stood at the central pivot of the garden discussing this, he walked off in a fury, and Mrs Rencoret told me that she wept. Then he weakened. He made a large garden for her roses only and, for the rest, he had his way.

RENCORET GARDEN, SANTIAGO

The garden is the mind of the house
Music is playing
So the garden is humming
A little tune.

The floor of the verandah
Is of petrified polished wood
So that the garden can remember
Its history.

A square of white roses
In a green line of box
Is the garden's flag
That it flies for peace.
I was walking in the garden
when the unicorn joined me
Wearing a collar of shards of crystal,
Silver and pearls.
Its complexion pale.
The unicorn blinked once or twice
Then drifted away
Into some dappled shade

Two gardeners stood bowing
And smiling—Pierrots,
Who, let's not forget
Do all the work.
Maids in pink uniforms were butterflies
Serving us tea.
Juan Grimm stood at the axis
Of the garden's world
The King of Spades who had
To give in to the Queen
Who like every girl wanted roses

Spring

In her old age as well as her youth—
Hard, perhaps, for a king to understand.
On the verandah I sat in a big cane chair
and Mrs Rencoret, wearing shoes like the Queen's
shook my hand.
Hers, soft as a horse's muzzle.
Finally we left
And the unicorn appeared from the shade,
Climbed into our bus
And we drove away.

(Sue Forge is the unicorn in the poem.)

Now their garden is softer, more feminine, and somehow more humane, because there are some flowers where, had Grimm had his way, there would have been none. It may not have the haute minimalism of his later work, but this is beautiful and civilised. A woman can take her secateurs and a basket and bring in roses for the house.

In Chile, families build houses for their children all around their property, a bit like some farmers in our country. But these houses are in the suburbs and an enormous central garden links the lot. Single people like Juan Grimm can hang their house from a cliff edge and garden to the edge where it falls down to rocks and sea. A circular swimming pool without a fence lies like a blue eye looking up at the equally blue sky. And, below, the sea beats on the rocks.

You cannot tell where garden ends and pure nature begins. The whole thing is wild and yet very strict and formal. That, I suppose, is the secret and why it is so breathtaking. It's like nothing else on earth. You don't know whether you are in love, or in shock, or simply hypnotised.

Perhaps gardens need an element of shock. There's a lot of talk about keeping mystery in a garden by never letting a person see where a path is going. But that's not what I mean. I mean the sort of shock where you see something that you have not only never seen before, but also have never thought possible. It shakes you up. Of course, art and some people can affect you like this. It only takes one glance, and you're done for.

Monday, 16 November

Soon after dawn I woke and watched the sky swept with lilac clouds and, below, the strelitzia seemed on fire with orange flames.

The night was hot. Watering the garden, I was weeding as I went, pulling out couch grass and flinging it backwards rather like the blackbird I complain about.

The sweet peas' leaves turned yellow yesterday and below them the beans are green. I am saving seeds from these sweet peas, the white ones most especially, because when I showed Paula a wedding in a magazine, she said, 'Oh! There's no such thing as white sweet peas!'

I said, 'Come with me.' And showed her.

This is the first time I've had good sweet peas and even though it's hard to buy the seeds of the tall ones, we can all have plenty of them now.

Spring

Last week, as I rode towards Peter and his wife, Helen's, house, I caught a whiff of her sweet peas. Hers are burgundy, navy blue, white, lavender and pink, and she told me that she thinks the darker the pea, the stronger the scent. Yet, these white ones smell. I mention these things not to debate but just because the question seems intriguing and the evidence is inconclusive.

On the matter of scent, this is the time when the streets are full of it. The cedar trees are massed with flowers, tall native frangipani are covered in yellow blossom and jasmine hangs over the railway station fence in a great white spill, a wave which can be smelt at the station and even at the crossing further down.

The two Tahitian lime trees give out their scent as I walk down the side path of the house and, from time to time, I pause and sniff and reluctantly knock off a few tiny fruit to give the tree a better chance. But, having a bet both ways, I leave a few.

Wednesday, 18 November

On another matter, last week I went to Gawler, which is about 25 kilometres north of Adelaide, to help my niece Stephanie, an interstate truck driver, make a dry garden around her century-old stone house. The exhilaration of working on somebody else's garden is one of the pleasures of old age. Once, I would have been hard put to work on my own and in fact, I was more than fifty before I did a tap of work in any garden that I can remember. It may be that gardening creeps up on one when some of the fury of youth falls away. Aristotle did say that enduring the sexual urges of youth is like being chained to a madman. One of the unsung boons of gardening is that no matter how obsessed one becomes, no matter

63

how much money is spent, how many hours spent slaving, respect is accrued in a way that almost nothing else but sacrifice of the highest kind kindles. Nobody ever says disapprovingly, 'Oh, she's a gardener!' Even if the garden is hideous, respect, however grudging, is there.

Speaking of hideous gardens, it is curious how different some gardens are that Lindy and I like. Today, walking back from the beach after a tai chi class with Lindy, I saw a woman with a hose under some old ti-tree in her front garden which is full of soft grey shrubs. I called out, 'I love your garden!' Now this lovely old shady patch is, to me, entirely beautiful but Lindy doesn't like it. Sometimes we like the same gardens, sometimes not.

On the matter of shade, I face the truth that there is barely a scrap of shade in the whole of my front garden. The two olive trees give a little, but will need a year or two more to provide much. The two shallow birdbaths need shade to keep them cool. I saw a pair of Murray magpies rise up from the blue ceramic bowl this morning when I opened the door, scattering water where they had been bathing. The persimmon is doing well and gives a small umbrella of shade around its trunk. Other than that, the sun blasts down and only a sarong shelters a withering tomato which has come good since it has had this shade.

I do hope you are not tired of the sparrows. Today, at 38 degrees, there was a lull in the feeding in the early afternoon when I went to lie on the pillows. I thought, for a while, the birds must be dead. But no, a sparrow flew up, entered and flew off. Later, I saw what looked like a yellow beak emerging from the hollow. Oh, at last, the young bird is coming to get a breath of coolness and perhaps to look around, measure the distance from the ground and consider its options. But later, no matter how long I stood on the porch staring up, there was no movement, so it seems that the yellow is a bit of straw or twig stuck there.

Is it oxytocin that keeps the pair feeding their young hour after hour in the heat? Perhaps they have nested there for seasons. It is unusual to have this heat in November so this is an arduous time for the birds. Oxytocin, that powerful chemical which keeps us devoted to our children and, sometimes, to others not so suited. And it is an irony I find amusing that while adult children have it for their own children, they do not have it for their parents. That is nature. Jane recently quoted another friend who said, 'I'd like to get my hands on the person who said that your children will be a comfort in your old age.' No, I'm not meaning my own children, only that I see how connected we are to sparrows.

Recently, another friend said that it was very sad that their eighty-year-old friend had to go into care. And I said, 'I don't find that very sad, if you don't mind me saying so. She's had a wonderful life; her children are healthy; her husband is healthy; she had plenty of money, could have what she wanted; lived wisely and now has come to the end of a fulfilled life.' Then I told her that what I found sad is our mutual friend Alexandra's mother's life. Her husband fought at Gallipoli, came back an alcoholic, and left her and their seven children for another woman. She reared those children alone and two sons went to the Second World War and died. 'Now that's what I call sad.'

Thursday, 19 November

At dawn, a lilac sky; lower down swept with palest lemon. No birds at all in that hour, even though the light was there, palely.

The first bird appeared at five to six (it is daylight saving) and then, while I waited anxiously for the sparrow pairs to arrive, none did until six-thirty. The nest's mouth had no straw or beak protruding, either blown off in the night or flown off. I walked over to the base of the pole to see if there was, perhaps, a bird fallen from the nest. No, there were none. Then at last, a sparrow entered. It would not enter, surely, if those birds inside were dead. At the other end of the beam, a sparrow entered that hollow, too, so it seems they have survived another day. Though now the heatwave is due to last another week.

How the parents love the shade. Every time one flies up to the pole, it shelters in the shade of a white ceramic transformer, going to and from the hollow. They love the shade like tennis players who, in the heat, walk back and forth into the shade every chance they get and then go out into the blaze to serve. I'd turn the hose up there if I thought that it would help. Peter, I see, hoses down his chook pens every hour or so while the hens stand panting in the heat. Poultry hate heat as citrus hate wind.

Standing on the low cliff top after a swim I kept thinking that with the pale blue glassy sea, there must be dolphins and suddenly there were. A pod of five or more slowly going south, up and down like hurdy-gurdy horses in the water. I called and pointed and people stopped and stared and then went on their way, better for the sight.

Later in the day I bought marigolds, eight pots to put around the tomatoes to stop the nematodes. All those, both seeds and seed-lings, which I planted weeks ago have failed. Recently, Jane said, 'Oh! I am buying French marigolds!' And you would think it was oriental liliums she was speaking of from the delight in her voice. I now am keen to have a lot. Crossing at the railway line, when the bells stopped, on my bike laden with the pots in flower, I thought that if a train came by, there'd just be marigolds and blood, which sounded like the title of a 1950s novel set in Mexico.

Riding down this street I saw the line of Stobie poles and realised the blazing obvious: that if two pairs of birds nest in the pole outside my house, there must be dozens more doing just the same in every suburb. I stared up at each pole and saw that some cross-beams were made of wood and some of iron which did not form a hollow, but all the others had the hollows that the birds needed. There must, therefore, be birds nesting in these poles across the entire city and along the country roads. Thousands and thousands of nests, when I had thought there was only this one outside my door.

We have all these connections with other living things and sometimes don't know it. 'We're nothing special!' Peri said to me, on another matter recently. A lesson I keep learning.

Soon, I am going out with a glass of wine, to plant the marigolds to let them have a few hours in the soil before tomorrow's heat.

Friday, 20 November

A cooler dawn with drifts of pale pink clouds lying horizontally above the pale lemon air.

At half-past five, a great twittering in the unnamed tree out the front. There must be nests in there. Earlier a sparrow flew up to the beam and entered. Life continues in that high-up nest. I see now, this obsession of mine is a sort of Hitchcock's *Rear Window*, with sparrows as the subject. I must get binoculars.

Nothing yet has died in the heat and 40 degrees is expected on Sunday. That will be the eighth day straight of more than

35 degrees. Officially, a heatwave and the first one for November since recorded data. I wanted a dry garden, a garden for the heat, and now I have one.

Exhilarated, I went out and mowed the lawn wearing a mask. The dust flew up in brown clouds and storms of dandelion fluffy seeds spread around. I like a yellow lawn in the summer. It looks natural and right.

If you want green lawns in summer, go to Chile. Oh, as I've said, how they waste water there. But they won't always have it.

The ambient heat from the cement where the shed once stood is being muffled by the two glory vines which day after day creep closer to the back door. The two 'Thompson Seedless' grapevines are too newly planted to give shade yet. I inherited a cement and gravel garden at the back of my house and now it's clear how white stone blazes in the sun and throws heat up.

Lately, there's a daily sight I love of bathers swinging, drying, on the plum tree's branch.

Saturday, 21 November

A black calligraphy of the Norfolk Island pine is outlined by the lilac sky at dawn. What does this signify? Faith, hope, endurance? It means anything I want it to mean. And any of those would be my choice.

Again, I watched and timed the sparrows. Just before seven, a great haste of mating, twelve times, until I lost count. At ten to three this afternoon, just as I had thought it was all over, a flurry of activity, two parents came and entered the hollow several times.

A friend who was staying overnight and I went to the nursery in our bathers and sarongs. As she had a car, we loaded up with pots of Christmas lilies and blood and bone. Beauty and the beast. I was tired of waiting until the cool change came, so I planted everything, including lettuce, down the side and sheltered these with cabbage leaves left from the glut there's been. Everything newly planted got a dose of Seasol from the watering can and a sprinkling of lawn clippings to protect them. I laid towels over all and came inside, my clothes radiating heat like a bull. It is to be, they say, 40 degrees tomorrow, so may heaven keep things safe.

Monday, 23 November

The cool change. It came and went this morning in a few hours and then the temperature rose to 31 degrees. A gardener on the radio said that it is better to water tomatoes before a heatwave rather than during. How long can they wait? I disregard this advice and pour the water from the shower onto them.

Today the premier announced water restrictions have been lifted somewhat. Now people can water thrice a week from six to nine in the morning and from six to nine at night. Half the people in a research interview said that they disregarded the restrictions. It does seem mad to let your garden die when stormwater runs out to sea.

However, the news on the sparrows is good. So riveting do I find these two nests and the life and death struggle going on that I can't lower the bedroom blind for any length of time, but am forced to lie staring from dawn onwards and much of the day, too, until the light grows. More feeding went on today than ever before. Twice, something yellow poked out of the hollow; surely it must be a beak. Then, a feather or a fledgling; too far up to see clearly. Twice a bit of straw dangled there. These birds may, perhaps, be dismantling the nest as they grow out of it.

I wonder how long it takes to rear sparrows. They may have been fed for days before I noticed the parents flying in. Any day now the moment may come when a bird looks out of the hollow and makes the leap and flight is the result. Or a plummeting. How do they know when? Do the parents refuse them food? Do they simply long to get away? How do they know how to fly?

Friday, 27 November

The jacarandas bloomed last week in a wash of that wonderful blue. One day the trees were black sketches in the sky and the next time I looked, the trees were clouds of blue. Today, in a cool sea breeze I walked over to the railway station where there are four or five trees and watched. Flowers fell like blue snowflakes in the soft wind. These small bells have an edge of five scallops at the end, are almost white inside with six minute ice-white stamens hidden in there.

Yesterday it was 50 degrees in the shade by my thermometer under the plum tree near the back door and it seems that this heatwave means the flowers are falling early. Jacarandas in bloom show it's exam time, with melting biros writing the answers. Once I lived in a street, Swift Avenue, Dulwich, in Adelaide, which was lined on both sides with jacarandas. Unless you have seen this sight, it is useless to try to describe it. There were two children and a husband and I thought it would always be so. You could say the blooms fell early there, too.

Joanie and I were talking the other day and I told her that I think old age is a chance for my redemption. You may have made a mess of your earlier life or many mistakes but now is the opportunity for redemption. I'm putting my shoulder to the wheel. She said she didn't agree and that I had nothing to be ashamed of but others had. This is an example of her iron loyalty that chains wouldn't break. After all, when I opened my eyes in the Royal Adelaide Hospital after a suicide attempt and found my wrists tied to the bed and a drip in my arm, it was Joanie in uniform standing before me saying, 'Katie, blow your nose.'

I said, 'I can't,' so she took a tissue and wiped it for me. And for forty years, without being asked, kept this event to herself.

I have been out planting beetroot and apple cucumber seedlings down the side and in the front garden. Ironically, the punnet of cucumbers was crushed when Stephanie Alexander's *The Kitchen Garden* fell out of the bike pannier as I brought it home from the library. I had to stop riding so that I could go back and collect the book, which meant the bike fell over and the seedlings were snapped off, all but one. I have planted them all, nonetheless, and we shall see.

Saturday, 28 November

Parma violets! Of all finds, today, pulling out couch grass, I saw, hidden at the base of an orange daylily, these violets I had thought long lost. I must have planted the daylily over the ruins of the violet and the lily may have shaded it and brought it back to life. It feels like a triumph, because the last thing I expected would be a double mauve parma violet lasting in the heat.

Wonderful how a cool change alters everything and all things seem possible. Fed up with the ailing orange tree, I pulled it out, washed the roots, which were more like Shirley Temple's curls than those of a healthy tree, and plomped it in beside the other orange tree. I lugged up a heavy piece of wire and threw it over the replanted lettuce plants which the blackbird had dug up. Capsicum had self-seeded from compost around a cumquat tree and I put them in beside the lettuce. I could have weeded all day.

All five of the citrus on the western side had a dose of pest oil. I pulled off all the fruit and flowers that I could find to give the trees a better chance. Then I remembered the word for the scent of citrus flowers which, for a month or more, I had tried to think of. Neroli. Neroli at night and neroli in the morning. My hands smell of neroli.

On the Meals on Wheels round, almost every client told me that more heat was coming. When we set out on our rounds, we are advised, as they say in hospitals, to 'push fluids'. When I urged one old man to protect himself by drinking more, he said, 'I never drink water.'

We have all become afraid. This evening, the first ever catastrophic red alert bushfire warning has been given for parts of the north of the state. It means that most people in the danger area must leave their homes before tomorrow morning. This warning system has been in place since people lost their lives in the Victorian fires last summer. Haystacks have imploded and, in the first fire, a farmer lost six million dollars worth of hay.

Summer

Thursday, 3 December

Seeds of orange cosmos which I planted on Sunday are already greening the seed box. Soaking them in warm water before sowing may have been helpful, that and warm weather. My niece, Annabel, has found a chook house for me and is using this hot day to paint it white. (She found it, a dog kennel, in Llewellyn Street dumped beside a railway line.)

At half past three this afternoon, while I was idly watching from my pillow, a sparrow emerged from the hollow beam, hopped onto a wire, looked about a while and went back in. Now this has never happened before. (The birds simply fly up, enter and then emerge after a few seconds; a minute or two at most.) The sparrow came out again, hopped around, returned and then *lo!* a long sweep down at about a 25-degree angle into the shrubbery. On the worst day, at the worst time, the fledgling left.

I was naturally electrified. (Imagine Jimmy Stewart putting down his binoculars and swallowing once or twice at what he thinks he has just seen.) Was this the first flight I have been waiting for? Truly, watching the Wright brothers would not have been more thrilling to me. Then, a few minutes later, another bird flew up and stayed in the beam for a longer time. That may mean that even if one has flown the nest, another remains to be fed. In future summers, even if the temperature is 43 degrees, there will be no need to worry because I now know that the heat on the iron beam will not kill the chicks.

Wednesday, 9 December

Diana Wood Conroy, my Wollongong friend who is an artist, writer and archaeologist now retired from teaching, rang this morning. She has taken up studying Greek theology in Sydney to keep herself alert and to investigate one of her interests. She told me some time ago that there are several young men in the class studying to become Orthodox Greek priests. They are from Lebanon, Serbia, Syria and Romania.

'Also,' she said, 'there are a few young women who are in Orthodox choirs or are interested in pastoral care. There's a limited role for women. I am by far the oldest. The lecturer is Romanian, a famous scholar—very dynamic and electrifying. Everybody wants to meet him.'

This, in part, is what she said today when I asked how the studying was going.

'I'm writing an essay on a letter written by a bishop to a nun, Xenia. (It means "Stranger" and it may not have been her real name—very few women are mentioned at this time, the 1340s.)

Gregory was the archbishop of Thessalonica in the last days of the Byzantine Empire. It was a long letter to this nun. He had revived the discipline of quietness.

It's related by some to a mantra—you recite a prayer, 'Jesus Christ, Son of God', over and over. It's very simple and it's used to quieten and dull the mind from other noise.

'It was a time of the High Renaissance, so Orthodoxy was being challenged you see, by Humanism. I love it because he used metaphors of gardening—husband, vine, tending it in all weathers. It's very beautiful.

'It's related to all the mosaics I love so much, full of plants, flowers and gardens. Would you like to read my essay?

'I don't mention this study—people think it is very off and not very useful. It's not very useful, is it?'

I said, 'But it is beautiful and lots of beautiful things are not useful.'

She went on, 'Yes, but if I mentioned studying the Baha'i religion, or someone like Kali, they'd be interested and if I mentioned the Virgin Mary, they'd go very quiet.'

'I know exactly what you mean, Diana. I did not ever mention riding to church in *The Waterlily* because I felt it would put some people off the book. Yet, soon after it was published my friend B. wrote a similar book with her Buddhist practice in it and had not a critical remark made as far as I know. But then, Buddhism is looked on as, perhaps, something intriguing and admirable to investigate. And no doubt it is.'

We said goodbye and I walked into the kitchen where the radio was broadcasting an interview on chaplains in schools. The amount of prejudice and the grilling of the man who was defending and explaining the practice was astounding. You would think the chaplains taught witchcraft.

To have faith or some spiritual life taught nowadays seems almost tantamount to teaching necrophilia.

Thursday, 10 December

Yesterday I picked the first rosemary from the two bushes grown from cuttings I snatched hanging over a fence. These tiny successes do not seem insignificant when there were about twenty cuttings stuck into the honey pot and planted out. Of course, I could buy rosemary in a pot but apart from the creeping 'Blue Lagoon' rosemary it gives more pleasure to get a cutting which I heard recently is, of course, a true clone of the mother plant.

And on clones, hear this: Jane has bought me a pot of rosemary grown from a cutting taken, it is said, by a digger from Gallipoli. (Did he keep it in a jar of water in his cabin all the way home?) Pots of this are sold by the Unley City Council. My grandfather fought at Gallipoli and, luckily, was taken off in a boat with jaundice. When I showed his great-great-grandson, Jack, the Gallipoli landing boat on display at the Australian War Memorial when he was about twelve, nothing would convince this boy that it was a real boat used at the Gallipoli landing. He said, 'They wouldn't use the real one.'

Now, a further report on the sparrows. For another week or more, even after I believed I had seen one of the young fly down to the garden, the parents went in and out as usual. Then they stopped. And what an enchantment it was to watch, day after day. Mesmerising to see the devotion.

Saturday, 12 December

Two months ago, my friend Peri sent me a return ticket to visit her at Mosman in Sydney. We walked through the botanical gardens as we often have. The size of the great trees above us made me see how different our botany is in Adelaide. Of course we have huge trees, but in the suburbs where I live and ride there is nothing to match those trees. The bark, the symmetry of some, the enormous branches covering huge lawns. I think we live too small. Too afraid. See a big tree, get it lopped. Easy for me to talk: I do not have to consider the fear of the roof caving in on a hot or windy day. We enjoyed those trees like a pair of old connoisseurs feeling ourselves almost as old. And happy. Yes, though I wonder how many times we will be able to do this walk and which will be the last one.

I love the way Peri takes my arm and we walk on together pointing and she says, 'I must go round to The Friends after this and see if they will sell me some (or one) of those.' Though not, in this case, to buy a seedling of one of the trees, as she already has those by the hundred on her farm near Currumbin.

Her garden in Mosman is entirely private, ruled over by walls of palms which she planted thirty years ago to keep her family from the public eye. We talked about our feelings on ageing as we walked. We are comfortable enough with the feeling of invisibility that has arrived. And we know we are the lucky ones as we are healthy so far and strong in the legs and back. (This sounds like a horse sale.)

It is Peri and Nan Evatt who taught me to garden. Not by telling very much, although they always answered questions. But I watched them and watched their gardens when they were not in them. I wanted to know what they knew and wanted to have what they had. Both these women had been gardening for thirty years when I met them. I think that many women learn to garden from their mothers.

My mother was too busy sewing and cooking early on, and then later, cooking, ironing twenty-eight shirts a week for my three brothers and my father, as well as running a poultry farm. She had to abandon sewing, having been, as she said, 'sewed out' like Coco Chanel. She was good at planting hedges (this eternal need for privacy is a theme, I see now). The first hedge was from plumbago cuttings from the garden of Gwen, my husband's mother. The next was of dark prunus alternating with blue plumbago.

CHRISTMAS (1)

Many have made their puddings and cakes
while I am happily awaiting my instructions.
Rain is never promised now, only showers
and that proves accurate—although Lindy and I
never give up putting out our buckets
in hope.

It's a time of less opulence than usual
and somehow it feels more decent
and dignified. The new fig tree has
twelve green figs.
Yes, the days of Christmas.

Summer

And soon, like others I am flying
to my dear ones though one is missing
and is beyond persuasion
although we always hope.

2010

Summer

Friday, 15 January

Three red pullets laid for my birthday. My son, Hugh, made a pen outside the kitchen window. He and his wife Cathy and their two daughters have come to stay. Peter, seeing that the yard was ready, took my granddaughters Claudia and Sophia and me to buy the poultry at his feed supplier. There was nothing fancy about the choosing. Cages of turkeys left over from Christmas, with electric fans blowing on them, ducks with yellow ducklings, exotic breeds of roosters and hens, two or three to a cage were in the shed. My brother strode past all of these, walked into a pen of dozens of red pullets, caught three and came out carrying two against his chest and one by its legs. Claudia walked beside, begging him not to hold the bird upside down. They were put into a cage in the back of the four-wheel drive with six bales of straw for the floor of their pen, along with a bag of special feed for layers.

Ignoring the fine set of wooden kitchen cupboards filled with straw and the dog kennel Annabel gave me (with two old bike baskets lined with straw for nests), the pullets prefer to sit and nest under three old umbrellas. They laid three soft-shelled eggs and then for days nothing more. Heat can put them off the lay, Peter says, so I thought no more of it.

One day a pullet collapsed before the sun came up so it was not heat and when I found her, ants were crawling over her head and her eyes were closed. I brought her inside to the laundry and left some water beside her (as she seemed unable to walk). Lindy looked at her and said she seemed to be dying then we went to the beach. Four hours later, we found the pullet up on her feet and she had eaten the food I left for her.

Later in the day Peter came to put the pullet out of her misery and we found her pecking away, quite recovered—and behind the door, an egg. Was it the first egg she had laid and was it so difficult to achieve, because the egg pressed, perhaps, on a nerve and paralysed her leg? That same hour Jodie, Peter and Helen's daughter, gave birth to a daughter in France, so Peter thinks the bird went out in sympathy with Jodie in her labour.

I put the hen, which I think had become bored, back in the pen at dusk and there has been no sign of trouble. Since then, finding no more eggs, I moved an umbrella and there, in a cardboard box under a black umbrella which Claudia had put in the pen, were seventeen eggs.

Jane brought me a lion's paw shrub called *Leonotis leonurus* so we walked out to the front garden and planted it between the two olives. Then, spurred on by the company, I planted out three boxes of orange and yellow cosmos seedlings I had sown, along with three pots of plectranthus (a type of grassy plant with a lavender pussy-tail flower which is hardy and drought proof). Jane watered those as I planted a yellow kangaroo paw, a plant I have never been able to grow.

We went off to lunch at Peter's. We had roasted drake which he had bred from an egg. All this urban farm stuff delights me greatly, as you can see. I long to be almost entirely self-sufficient. Big 'Mariposa' plums galore (most of which I did not know were on the netted tree) and a hat full of tomatoes daily plus two eggs. Now while that wouldn't keep a woman, it can help. And I aim for much, much more.

Monday, 25 January

Bunches of hot pink bougainvillea hang over fences in great drooping swags. Figs and pomegranates hang there, too. This is the opulence of Adelaide which amazed Peri when she came here one March for Writers' Week. She used to take the fruit back to her hotel: relishing it because she grew up in Rockhampton where there were only mangoes and bananas.

Peri is, as you know, one of the friends who taught me most about gardening. Every six weeks or so she goes to her orchard in Queensland. I never saw anyone love fruit so much. She walks in the orchard eating it as she goes. A friend through thick and thin.

Huge hibiscus and oleanders are in bloom in old gardens where the lawn, I am happy to say, is yellow and, while the original gardener may be dead or gone, the flowers brush against the eaves of houses. The reason I say that I like the yellow lawn is that it seems to be a better look for a dry climate. We are used to seeing green lawn as healthy, but now I think it is not healthy at all. In fact, it's sick.

As I ride to Glenelg on Sunday mornings (which is one of the days it is legal to water gardens before ten) old women are out in their dressing gowns watering a scrap of yellowing lawn. I feel like hopping off the bike and starting a bit of a crusade to talk them out of wasting their time. But it is a beautiful thing to stand with a hose in your hand trying to save something and I enjoy it myself, so I don't stop to preach.

Last week my friends Annie G., with whom I nursed, and her husband Brian came to lunch on the way to their holiday shack at Carrickalinga. I talked them into taking one of the cuttings of the old fig I took from a vacant lot. These cuttings now have not-quite full-sized leaves on them and are ready to plant out. As they say at the tennis, 'She's got nothing to lose!' (except the match of course). I mean, the fig cost nothing and it may live and outlast us all.

Later this week, I am taking two more of these cuttings, one to my brother Bill for his dry garden and the other to his daughter Stephanie at Gawler. So, with luck, there soon may be other fig trees around the country with that amazing ruby red fruit which the mother tree has, and which it is about to have buckets more of, in a month. And all it took was some cuttings in late spring when the branches already had leaves on them.

They were dipped in farm honey and stuck into an old plastic pot with cheap potting mix in it. The farm honey, I read, is useful for sprouting cuttings because it has not been sterilised as is the case with honey sold in shops. Some say honey is better for striking cuttings than the special hormone powder bought from nurseries. Others use Vegemite in solution. Some, of course, use nothing and which are the best of these I can't say. I stick to the honey because it is given to me by Tucker, who lets an apiarist keep his hives on his property and in return he is given plastic buckets of honey. The honey has different flavours depending on what the bees feed on in the native scrub—melaleucas, acacias or the scrubby gums.

When Hugh, his family and I went down to stay at Tucker's property, 'Ninga Ninga', near Robe, last Boxing Day, there had been a bushfire a kilometre or two from the main homestead. Bees had made a hive in a huge old gum and the fire had half-destroyed the tree. Where the bees went, Patricia, my sister-in-law, did not know but she said that sometimes she could not use the road to visit their son Ben because the bees would attack her. Then she had to drive overland through paddocks. Why would bees attack her? I didn't ask, but she would know. I will ask her later today. (I have the answer. To pass the tree with the hive, Patricia had to open a gate and would have no defence against the bees.)

Two days after we left, I rang to see if the fire was out (because it had been flaring up again on some nights when the wind rose, as the roots and the inside of tree trunks smouldered for days). Patricia said a man with a water pump on his ute was going round putting out small fires. She went on to say that their younger son Angas had no electricity on his property because bees had nested in the electrical box at his farmhouse. The men from the electricity company could not approach the box until a man came and smoked the bees out.

About ten years ago, bees invaded a perfectly good two-storey house on the property and were so dangerous that, in the end, Tucker had to burn the house down, billiard table and all. One more bee story and I'm done. Once Tucker, chased by a swarm of bees, was saved when he stopped, lay on the ground and tossed sand over himself.

Now, of course, I'm wondering if I could have a hive in the garden and continue this self-sufficiency theme. There are lots of flowering trees on the land opposite here and most of them are natives, and there are all those hibiscus and oleanders everywhere. But I suspect a hive might be illegal in the suburbs.

It is a family trait to take things a bit too far, or at least, further than would be thought normal. For instance, last week Peter brought home two Gouldian finches which he found at the feed store. These were the first Gouldian finches he had ever seen and he was smitten by them. The feed store owner told him they were the last two he had as the birds' breeder had moved to live in a caravan park where pets were banned. These exquisite little birds are currently threatened in the wild but are common as pets. Now Peter has built a huge aviary and has a tall dead tree branch standing in it, with a dozen finches which he bought since he fell in love with the first pair. He is going to breed them and sell them to that feed store owner.

Saturday, 30 January

It is addictive to count seedlings as they appear out of the flat black dirt. From hour to hour there are more. I count six sunflowers, and three hours later, count eight. If I went out now, there could be more. This morning, inspired by these seeds, I made two more seed boxes, soaked lettuce, tomato and zucchini seeds, and sowed them. Too late, I remembered reading that lettuce needs a cool temperature to sprout so, because it is more than 30 degrees, I laid a towel on top of the box and wet it. All this mucking about with seeds is beguiling, costs almost nothing and sometimes has thrilling results.

Counting is, I think, a certain kind of obsession which can get out of hand. I had an Aunty Olive who, on her deathbed, counted and as I stood listening she added and subtracted. It is, I suppose, a graceful, energetic way to die. At the time, I thought how interested she was in all those numbers. I think this may run in the family. I see I have a goodly dose of this myself with plums, eggs and seedlings. Do I count clouds? No. The bounty of the sky is there day after day but I never count when I look up, not unless it is three seagulls flying over.

Yesterday, I went with Stephanie to a succulent nursery at Kapunda. It is in the grounds of an old evangelical Lutheran church which was built in 1907, and is now a dwelling. Nearby is another bigger Lutheran church in a beautiful small town full of stone houses and grand churches. This church, I think, was another strand of Lutheranism but, even so, the churches of the town were all built with money from the copper mines. This difference interested me because our family fled Germany because of religious persecution. But, why, I used to think, would they have been persecuted in the nineteenth century when Lutheranism was well established there? The answer was that there were two types and one overcame the other. All the towns around the Barossa were filled with migrants who came because of religious persecution and it is these people who filled the Barossa with vines.

Stephanie bought a load of succulents and we drove back to her home to plant them in the new dry garden we'd made the day before. I planted eleven agaves from my garden and built a small path in the dust for her to walk on. Earlier, with her electric scissors (which are a sort of chainsaw), she cut down a dead may bush while I held the branches. New to me, they are the sort of scissors you use when you are not dressmaking.

Then her boyfriend dug the old bush out with a crowbar. Later they planted a new hybrid, thornless, scented, lilac bougainvillea to climb up the trellis. The two grapevines which we planted on my last visit are growing nearby, lush and green.

I am mad about this garden. Everything needs to be done. It is so dry that when you dig, the dust rises and sticks to your face. Next day you cough.

Wednesday, 3 February

This afternoon, the phrase 'the beauty of the despised' was on a piece of paper among invoices I was sorting to do my tax. It has been going over in my mind, as these things do, like an old song. I see now that it sums up the fate of many of the plants sown early in the life of the colony which became disdained over the years and are now cultivated. For example, Jane had a long search for that old lion's paw plant which grew outside lavatories in country towns. Earlier I would have sneered at the prickly aloes and, to be frank, half the succulents in the front garden. And, figs. Annabel has just left and she pointed out, when I showed her the fig cuttings leafy in their pot and the three trees here, that figs, once despised, are now $24 a kilo at Mr Caruso's, the Glenelg greengrocer.

Of course, the most despised fruit of all was once the quince, and now people treasure them. There is also the loquat but that, I think, is a special case and only some people love them. But

Annabella Boswell, in her nineteenth century diary, wrote that at Port Macquarie in New South Wales she made loquat jam. (That people had so little fruit in the early life of the colony I attributed to the fact that they had not yet had time to plant fruit trees.) A friend told me she made loquat chutney last week and I could barely suppress a shudder. Another friend, Annette, told me she tried cooking quinces but they didn't turn red. She said she thought she'd have another go but I said, 'There was no need, all you had to do was leave them on the heat for another hour or two.' Today I made Annie G.'s, one of the nurses, recipe for baked quinces. It's for one of our regular nurses' lunches—there are ten of us and we meet in each other's homes about every six weeks. The recipe says roast four quinces after wiping them with a wet cloth (you never need to peel quinces), halving them and covering them with a cup and a half of water, one cup of sugar, a quarter of a cup of honey, some cinnamon and the juice of a lemon. With the quince halves face down in a baking pan, covered with baking paper, roast for two hours at 180 degrees Celsius. They should become ruby red. A tiny, and I mean tiny, bit of rosewater on top and they are done. They are good with Greek yoghurt and honey. (Four quinces would serve eight. I treble this for ten so there are leftovers.)

If you would like to make an easier alternative to quince cheese, my friend Biffy, another of the nurses, gave me her recipe, which saves a lot of work and I like it better.

Take half a litre of water and the same of vinegar and mix in a saucepan with one kilo of white sugar and the zest and juice of two lemons. Let simmer until well mixed. While this is happening, line two baking trays with baking paper.

Cut six or more quinces (depending on size) wiped, not peeled or cored, into slices about one quarter of an inch (half a centimetre) thick. Simmer these in the syrup until pink. (They will grow red later in the oven.)

Remove quince from syrup, drain in a strainer, keeping the jelly-like syrup to use with stewing apples or to pour on ice-cream.

Lay the slices out separately on the trays and bake in a slow oven (about 100 degrees Celsius) for two hours or so until red and cooked through.

Check that the slices do not burn as they cook, as they can catch easily. Allow to cool. Peel off paper and store in lidded sterile jars. Serve with cheese.

QUINCES

Peri
yesterday we stood in a bookshop
I opened a book
there they were
quinces
pale green
luminous and furry

strange as green cats
so solid
they sit in the hand
heavy as the history
of quinces

Summer

remember the tree we saw
in the backyard at Cummins
we pulled up and stared

a laden tree
spectacular
against the galvanised iron fence
see
everywhere beauty arrives
unexpectedly
as that green snake
lying across our path
in the mottled bush light

once I brought you quinces
from the tree Gwen and I found
at McLaren Vale
she stood there
and she clapped her hands
like a child with a present

the tree stood
giving us green lamps
which we picked

I took them to you
and put them on a blue plate
you shook your head
and smiled

There they sat
this curious fruit
that cut has the texture
of wet chalk
and cooked
turns not like water to wine
but fruit into blood

On another matter, the cumquat hedge is wilting. Because on the morning of New Year's Eve, I spread three or four bales of straw on top of cardboard and newspaper around every little tree, thinking it would be shelter enough for them. I left them alone and until yesterday didn't see that they were suffering. These trees, which I planted with confidence and not a thought of any future difficulties, have been the hardest trees I ever grew. Perhaps it is the windy site, and perhaps it is the soil. Or just lack of water.

But Lynn Collins, who is a curator and knows a lot about colonial gardens, told me that when working at Vaucluse House in Sydney, there were three trees in a row and only one thrived. When they dug down and tested the soil, the tree that had flourished had quite different soil from the other two.

I think in the case of my cumquats, it may be that they are planted, those that face the railway line, on top of the ruins of an old stone fence. Those along the western side are taller and thicker and altogether different and this could be because they are sheltered from the wind by houses opposite and, perhaps, there is no archaeology below them.

Between them, in the two years they've been planted, they've consumed about six bales of hay and bags of manure. Some would say that the poor ones should just be taken out. But that's hard to do when you have cherished something. The trees, like a child, could deny me, but I cannot deny them.

Eighteen sunflowers are now up in the seed box and in another box, a swathe, a smattering of green, which may be parsley or tomatoes.

Thursday, 4 February

Rain in the night. Only a few drops, but people like Lindy and I have buckets and wheelbarrows out. When it rains heavily, Lindy goes out and drags a bucket through the rush in the gutter, garnering every bit she can. Once or twice, I've done it, too, even though you get drenched and look deranged harvesting the water like a homeless person at a bin. Need defeating shame.

A green spread of self-sown pumpkins has blocked the side path. These are 'Butternut' and 'Kent' which came from the compost. Last year the same thing happened at the back garden, the spread nearly reaching the back door. I didn't care to pull them out because at least it was greenery cooling the cement where the shed once stood. I never thought there'd be a harvest, but there was, and there is still one striped pumpkin left in the laundry.

There are three eggs a day now hidden in the straw behind the closed door of the old kitchen cupboard in the pen. The three other doors are open and now I see that chooks like secrecy and darkness. They enter through a door and go to the end where they like it best.

Stefano De Pieri, the Mildura cook, quotes the aphorism, 'Olive trees like silence, solitude and sun.' But while that sounds romantic, the fact is, they prefer water, fertiliser and sun.

I grew olive trees when I lived at Woonona near Wollongong. One of the three olives I planted reached the roof of the shed in a year. I had not known that there was an old septic tank where it grew. And, while the others in the garden outside the gate grew well enough for Greek people to come and ask if they could take some fruit, these gave nothing like the rain of olives falling from the tree at the shed. Same climate, different food. I rest my case.

Tuesday, 9 February

One or two flags of peachy orange canna flower wave outside my bedroom. I watch them from the bed now that the sparrows have abandoned their high iron nest. It is movement that catches the eye. When the sparrows left, I don't know, but for long afterwards I thought I saw the young fly down. Larger sparrows were still going in and out of the nest. It went on for another month or so which may mean that a second or third pair bred there.

This staring out of the window, which I find so pleasing lying here, is a sort of meditation, thinking almost nothing and feeling no pain or guilt. It is just a form of contemplation which can't, surely, be a waste of time. When Arthur Miller was married to Marilyn Monroe, he said that when he was staring out of the window his wife thought he was wasting time, but he said that he was working.

These tall, green and maroon-leafed cannas have taken no work and little water, yet have been one of the best flowering plants this summer. There are about twenty or more and, among a tall Mexican sage which waves beside them and which also takes no water, they look beautiful. I have looked up cannas in *Botanica* and it says that they are a native of South America and now are so hybridised there are few pure breeds. They grow beside creeks and on the way to Wollongong; I used to ride by a big stand of red cannas which had got into the bush.

Today is the second of 38-degree heat and tomorrow is due to be the same. I've had heat stroke so have been lying around, with ice in a towel on my head, off and on for three days. Hence, more than usual watching of those orange flags. Last summer, because so many of the elderly died in the heatwaves, the morgues ran out of room and refrigerated containers had to be used for the bodies.

I knew all that, and yet still went out and got 'a touch of the sun', as it is called. It used to be more common, and Tucker had a tremendous dose of heat stroke once during his cattle sale when he sat on railings and watched for hours without a hat. He was staggering down the verandah, Patricia said, when he came home.

He was staggering on another day when Patricia, on hearing his feet dragging, ran out to meet him. A jackaroo had strung up a wire to hang out his washing between two trees and Tucker had ridden a motorbike through it and cut his throat. He wouldn't be driven 60 kilometres to the doctor in Kingston, so lay down and got up when he felt better. He has worn a beard ever since, to cover the scar.

A grazier has decided to buy 5000 cattle from Tucker and Patricia and to truck them up north where there has been rain, around Bourke and Wilcannia. Patricia said today that the men have been drafting and weighing cattle for a week. They load 980 a day. The cattle go on trucks to Mildura, are put into a yard, fed hay and water, and then put on trucks and taken north. The gamble is, will there be enough grass to last before they can breed and the calves mature for a year? Drought does not only kill animals. Tucker told me at Christmas that recently two graziers near his places in the north have killed themselves. 'It is tough country,' he said.

Wednesday, 10 February

A wonderful day in the garden. I filled some old stone pots I had painted white with self-sown parsley which had been growing among the gravel in the back. Also, basil, lemon thyme, mint and dill went in. Two pot-bound English lavenders went into the holes left from digging soil for pots in the driest part of the front garden. Tomorrow I am going back to the nursery to buy more.

Last week I made my great-niece Chloe, who is twenty-four, a herb garden of eleven pots for her upstairs flat on Jetty Road, Glenelg. I enjoyed doing it and it made her so happy that I thought I'd make one for my new young neighbour, Barbara. She is English and had never seen an apricot tree before I showed her mine. She has a two-year-old son, Jack, who sometimes comes and collects the eggs from the chickens' nest.

Barbara's mother gave her a lemon tree in a black plastic pot for Christmas but it shed all its leaves. I found it baking in the sun at the front of her house and took a chance, brought it home, gave it seaweed solution and put a wet towel around the pot and now, only three weeks later, it is full of green leaves. When Barbara saw it last weekend (I had told her I'd taken her plant), the change was so swift that she asked if the tree was hers.

Friday, 12 February

Things I have learnt in the past year:

Stone fruits should be pruned immediately after the end of fruiting.
When I read this in Helen Young's column in *The Weekend Australian*, I ran out half-full of disbelief and chopped off the entire apricot tree's outer limbs to two-thirds of their size. Since then, I have heard of this elsewhere so last week, with more belief, when I undressed the 'Mariposa' plum of its white veil, I took off the limbs then and there, having just gathered the last of the fruit. I have been having them cold (after they've been halved with their stones left in, then fried cut-side down in just a dab of butter, and a cup or so of sugar and no water added) for breakfast with yoghurt.

A fig tree responds well to having its roots severed right around the outside of the branches' ends which is called the 'drip-line' of the tree.
It's true, I haven't done this yet, as it seems radical and risky, but I am gearing up to it.

And I learnt, in these past months, that one of the cuttings I made from the fig in a vacant lot in Glenelg is viable, as it has grown up to the roof outside the kitchen window and has green figs forming. Wondering if they would just be sterile clones, I sent a pot of new cuttings, now half a metre tall, to my niece-in-law Anita on a farm near Kingston in the south-east. It is a relief to know that they will fruit. This girl, about to marry my nephew Angas, is hungry for fruit trees. Curiously, there is an enormous sterile fig tree in their garden. It may be that there are no wasps around to fertilise it.

As you might recall, I have learnt that it is not bees but wasps which figs need. Yet why do the wild figs by the railway line here grow and fruit without any care at all? And why does the fig, given to me by Mr Perry and planted at my gate, now have figs ripening on it, after the note it came with said that it needed a 'Capri' fig to fertilise it? I rang Mr Perry to ask these questions and he explained that he gave me the fig because he wanted to know some of the answers himself.

All citrus trees need deep watering at the drip-line once a week, more in very hot weather.
This means that the cumquat hedge was a mistake to plant in what I had hoped was to be an almost drought-proof garden.

Also, I've found I was wrong about cannas not needing much water. They will survive with little, but to thrive they need extra water. This, I see now, is why they grow wild near creeks and waterways.

During heatwaves hens need to be dipped into a bucket of cold water when they collapse.
Peter said: 'Poultry can survive in temperatures up to that of their own body, which is 38 degrees. Anything above that, and they begin to struggle as they have few means of cooling themselves apart from gasping and fluffing out their feathers.'

So, during heatwaves, poultry need to be let out to sit in shade, preferably under a tree. If they collapse, they can be revived by plunging their bodies into a bucket of water for a couple of minutes. Their pen can be hosed every few hours if there is no means of letting them out. They don't much like it, but it will save them.

There are now foxes in the suburbs.
The postmistress lost a hen to a fox last week. An Italian man at the supermarket said his mother lost her entire flock to a fox a month ago. I told him to tell his mother that she had saved my hens because now I will make sure the gate to their shed is shut nightly.

I've been reading magazines and a book on poultry-keeping which is why, I think, I am writing this in the style of a guide.

Beginning sentences with 'It's terrible . . .' has a disheartening effect on others.
From time to time another friend, Shirley, a retired teacher before she died, and I used to go walking. The truth is, because she had undiagnosed depression and denied it when I had suggested it, sometimes it was hard not to feel drained. For instance, when her monologue became too hard to bear, I developed a technique to protect myself. I'd fall behind and remove my hearing aids and pop them into my bra. One day, when it was particularly harrowing, I saw a white bird flying high over the sea and said, 'Oh, look at that white bird, Shirley. I wonder what sort of bird it is. See the way it catches the light.'

She glanced up briefly and said, 'It's a seagull. They're filthy birds, full of lice.'

On another day, Shirley and I kept to the back streets on our walk to avoid the wind on the beach. We were in a part of town we hadn't been before, and found a magnificent *Magnolia grandiflora* in full bloom on a vacant block. As we ran towards it, I said, 'Oh, isn't this wonderful, Shirley?'

She said, 'It's terrible, you know. The flowers only last a day.'

It takes a certain kind of genius to kill a moment like that.

On the way home we came to the lights on Brighton Road and I said, 'Oh look, Shirley, the lights are green.'

'That doesn't happen very often.'

It is not much use hoping that sunflowers will self-seed when they spill their black bounty on the ground.

Ants come and take out the centre of the seed, leaving the black papery covering. It looks as if there are seeds aplenty there, but they are simply empty black shells.

Also, watch the flowers when the yellow outer petals begin to disappear because if you don't, the seeds will spill before you have cut off the head. Of course, if you don't want to save the seed for next season, or give it to poultry, there is no need to do anything except tug at the thick stem and pull the plant out when it has done its duty.

Talking about the price of food, or of things you dislike, makes you seem old.

Excuse me while I kill this fly.

I have discovered that if you see something you do not like, say a car, a house, a tree or a dog, and tell the person with whom you are walking or driving, it just pulls them down. (These things do not have a notice on them asking you what you think of them, nor do they ask that you tell somebody how much you dislike them, if, in fact, you do.)

Grapes and fruit of all kinds need to be netted before the fruit is sweet to save it from possums and birds.
I have just lost the first of the 'Thompson Seedless' grapes. Not that it matters much, but I would have liked to give them to friends.

Today my friend Peter Goldsworthy came with his wife Lisa Temple to breakfast and he took the net from the plum tree where it has served its purpose and draped it over the fig, having picked the first three big pink-centred figs which we ate for breakfast at the table under the vine. A plastic bag had saved those three figs from birds. One was so big and ripe it had burst. Figs will not ripen off the tree.

Stone fruit, though, will ripen off the tree but it will taste better if it can stay on until it is sweet. Then it will be delicious if eaten immediately. This is why stone fruit from the greengrocer has less flavour than fruit straight from the tree. It is not the grocer's fault.

If you are old enough, you may remember a film called *The Greengage Summer* in which Kenneth More and Susannah York were the leading actors, and in it they ate those same plums from the tree and I could not, as a teenager, understand why it was meant to be so special. But they were English people in France, I think, and they were not used to so much heat and bounty.

The final thing I learnt in the past year was that as you age, you are wise if you have your hearing tested.

I had found that when teaching I could not hear the person reading out their work at the back of the class. I asked the student sitting next to me if she could hear and she nodded. So, off I went to a hearing clinic and now I hear well, but not if I mislay my hearing aids. I have lost one now, so I must go and search.

Later: no luck.

I remember the amazing effect and my joy when I first had a hearing aid fitted and rode home with them in my ears from Wollongong to Woonona where I lived then, on the bike path by the sea. For the first time I could hear the tyres turning.

Then I found that silence has a sound. When hearing aids are removed, silence suddenly looms up like a noisy cloud. It is as if the air breathes. It is not one's own breathing, nor a heartbeat, there is nothing rhythmical to it; just the sound of the silence.

Monday, 15 February

Last week I sowed spinach, small cabbage, silverbeet, capsicum and beetroot seeds. Learning, learning, learning, I laid the remains of two red capsicums with the stem and seeds in the sun for two days to dry out and sowed them and, amazingly, they have sprung up in one of the three seed boxes: it cannot be anything else because they have such a recognisable leaf.

Tremendous havoc of floods in Queensland and Victoria means it will be difficult to buy vegetables for a while. Although Peter says he thinks not, as the silt pouring down onto the plains in the floods will fertilise the ground and soon it will be planted. But where did the silt come from? Somebody must have lost it.

Summer

Sunday, 21 February

On Friday it rained all day. I ran in and out as the green bin began to overflow with water from the gutter spout, bailing it out and flinging it on the fruit trees. Thrice I changed my wet clothes but it was a pleasure to do. The only reason I stopped in late afternoon was that I could lift no more buckets of water up and over the bin's brim. Later, when I'd had a couple of drinks, I went out and began again. I would like a rainwater tank and when I get a front fence I will begin to save for one. Into the wet soil I put four pieces of edible ginger rhizomes as I have always wanted to grow my own and with the floods in Queensland it will be hard to buy along with much else.

In one of the many coincidences that have happened lately, Joanie gave me six flowers last week and I found that they were mentioned in a book Peri lent me called *Sugarflower*. Never having seen or heard of angelonia, I looked it up and found that it is related to linarias, snapdragons and others. It belongs to the Scrophulariaceae family. Here, in the book by John Oakes about his late grandmother, Lucy North, a Queensland gardener, he mentions that her favourite flower was angelonia and it grows like a weed there.

On the matter of coincidence, I heard New York writer Paul Auster speak on radio about a true story of a student who went to Paris and found a room in which to live. Later the student was told by his father, when he gave him the address, that it was the same room in which a relative had hidden from the Nazis.

Well, I have a couple which perhaps can match that. Last month I was riding my bike to Jetty Road, Glenelg, where my great-niece Chloe had removalists in to unpack her furniture. I was laden with scones, cups, milk and tea for morning tea. Suddenly I remembered that I hadn't packed a teapot and I knew it was unlikely that Chloe would be able to find one among the boxes, even if she had one. It was too far to go back so I rode on for about five minutes, and there in the middle of the road was an old tin teapot. Nothing around it, no hard rubbish waiting to be collected on the side of the road, just the teapot. Think of something and it will appear. I told Chloe that I thought, and who wouldn't, that it was a good sign. We made the tea, heated the scones, spread them with butter and strawberry jam and, with the removalists, we ate up.

Now the second strange event. When my brother Bill's daughter, Stephanie, came to stay overnight a fortnight ago, she helped me lift the grapevine at the back door higher onto the wires hung for its support. As we heaved and lifted, Stephi turned a stick to tighten the wire around the vine, while I told her the story of the stone pots I had bought which had no holes in the base. I had only noticed this after I had made Chloe a herb garden of pots for the steps outside her flat. I said that I had to tip the plants out of the pots and make a hole for drainage with a screwdriver and a hammer. Stephi, being a truck driver and so knowing a bit about tools, said that what I had really needed was a drill. Then I saw something dark, hanging among the grapevine growing up the fence, and put my hand in and out came two rusted manual drills.

The third coincidence happened when I went to the shop to buy bread to make crumbs to stuff red capsicum with fried eggplant and onion, grated cheese, currants and chopped herbs, ready to bake. Before I went in, I looked for some greenery in the supermarket bin to give my chooks and saw there a strange cream-coloured vacuum-packed half-moon-shaped object. It looked a bit like a loofah for use in the shower. It was a package of breadcrumbs in perfect condition. I don't try to explain these events, but I think it is best to be careful (as the saying goes) of what you wish for. Unloving gods grant wishes. But in this case, the opposite.

Monday, 22 February

This morning I dug up couch grass in the front garden. It had grown through the newspapers and mulch I laid down when the garden began. There is nothing, as far as I know, that can defeat couch. Poison, maybe.

Seedlings of English spinach and capsicum from my seed box went in and I see now that the front garden will have so many vegetables it will look as if Italian people live here. I have always liked the look of their gardens. They are clever gardeners because their gardens feed the owners and their families.

When I see neighbours planting ornamental trees around their new houses, I struggle not to suggest plums, figs, apricots, almonds, anything that will thrive here with little help. I could wring my hands. If we can't buy oil in the future, the world will only have enough food for a few weeks and there will be famine.

Sunday, 28 February

Today, my twenty-two-year-old grandson, Jack, came to lunch. He is going to live with his mother in New York for a while. I was not looking forward to saying goodbye but it passed off easily enough as I walked him to the corner. Earlier, after lunch under the vine, we walked up the street to see the new houses being built in place of old ones which were mainly War Service houses like mine. Built for or by the men who came back in 1945. I was explaining to Jack that before the old houses were here, there were vineyards and almond orchards.

Across the road beside the railway line was a fig tree the council workers had pruned into a perfect wineglass shape and on it were ripe, ruby red-centred figs. I showed him how to twist them off without bruising the flesh and as we walked he ate and was amazed at the flavour. So now he knows. Further on was a pomegranate tree hanging over a fence so we took some of that fruit home, too.

At home, to keep moving and not let my sadness show, I went indoors and brought out secateurs and long pruning shears. Together we pruned off all the old growth of the blood plum which has just finished fruiting. It is the tree I brought home in a pannier on my bike and planted to pollinate the 'Mariposa' plum. Perhaps he will remember this in New York.

Lindy rang this evening, back from visiting her thirty-two-year-old son Robert's grave at Tanunda on the anniversary of his death. She said she had just been told that the fig is called the Tree of Life. This morning I gave her a dish of them from the tree at my back door still veiled in its white netting. As we walked around the garden, Lindy said she and her husband Robert had seen monarch butterflies in their own garden last week and at Tanunda. When their son died, an elderly Greek woman told Lindy that these butterflies visit after a death because they are the spirit or the soul of the one who has died. It comforted them considerably when they walked with their daughter Catherine on the beach the day after the funeral and a cloud of these same butterflies followed them on their walk. Lindy said, on telling me this when I came to live here, 'Have you ever seen butterflies at the beach?' No, I haven't.

Earlier this weekend Hugh and his family came from Sydney to stay for the same family wedding that brought Jack here. Claudia and I planted pink belladonna lilies along the side fence where the four planted a year ago are in full bloom. I told her that we call them 'naked ladies' because they bloom on a long stem devoid of leaves. It is only when the flower dies that the leaves appear. Jane, my old friend, and I remember driving between thousands of these flowers blooming wild on both sides of a road near McLaren Vale about thirty years ago.

Claudia kept saying, as I dug and then she tried, that the soil was terrible. It is true that it is hard there but I explained that it is the same soil which, on the other side of the fence, is growing big tomatoes and a heavy black oval eggplant so it can't be too bad. But she would have none of it. I was surprised at how defensive I felt of this lovely dirt into which I put so much work. We also planted 'Replete' daffodils around the persimmon tree in the front garden and I gave Claudia some to take home. She thought these very few compared to her order from Tesselaar Nurseries as she said that they are so cheap she ordered a lot. It depends on your income, Claudia, I thought but didn't say. Anyway, these are fancy daffodils with a peach-coloured frill.

Last year Claudia joined the Newtown Community Garden Club. She came home from her first visit with parsley, which she knows her father likes. She told Hugh, 'They are very political down there, Dad, but I don't say anything. I just garden.' I don't know if she is the only child there. Gardening with a child is enchanting.

My mother in her nineties used to say, 'Nouns elude me.' More and more they elude me, too. I have developed almost a speech impediment as I halt mid-sentence trying to think of a word. After a tiny pause, I say it. For years I could not remember echium (and now, still must pause before it comes back), the beautiful tall blue-flower spiked shrub which grows with almost no water.

Autumn

Thursday, 11 March

Yesterday morning when I shuffled into my sheepskin slippers for the first time this year, I knew it was autumn, whatever the date. There was a time when I would have laughed if anybody said that I would one day wear slippers. As you see, I do now and while the young and old wear ugg boots (suddenly fashionable in a way they never have been), I draw the line at them, though Jane tells me I am missing something.

There is something about the vulnerability of slippers. A pair lying straight together pointing under a bed shows sweetly, humbly, the commonality of us all. How we love comfort. We like warm feet. Once I saw a tyrant's slippers in his deserted palace and the same thing struck me. Nothing of his posturing from a balcony, or standing straight, wearing a fedora as his troops marched by, ever made him seem human. But his slippers did. This was Saddam Hussein; he left that pair behind when he fled.

I can see other signs of autumn. Yesterday afternoon, lying in the back sunroom reading, I looked up and saw the sun pouring through a ruby red vine leaf making it look like a piece of stained glass. Also, I've got the preserving bug. As I've said, I think this is some primitive instinct in some of us to prepare for winter. And what is this flurry of vegetable planting? Carrots, for instance. Why on earth do I want to plant carrots when they are so cheap and on sale all year round?

Lindy called in this afternoon with flowers from her garden. She said that the neglected old house which we pass sometimes on our walks is to be demolished and that the stinking lilies she wants are still there. She wanted us to go today with trowels to dig some up.

The demented woman owner (who is not older than us) has gone. The gutters sag, the fence is bent, the roof rusts, a cat slinks through the grass under the clothesline propped with a stick like a last fading hope. Often we have watched and wanted to get Lindy the lilies growing under a huge fig. I have no wish for the lilies as they have that immense stench. Lindy's garden, though, is a quarter of an acre so they can go by the furthest fence.

Previously searching for those lilies in the deserted garden, we had no luck. None to be seen nor any bulbs in the ground. But stupendous luck with naked ladies flowering in the chaos of a fallen fig tree riddled with tall buffalo grass. That time we had brought trowels and I dug up seven big bulbs. So urgent was my pleasure that they were planted with the others outside the green iron fence before I went into my house. Something for nothing has immense appeal, don't you find? Especially if you have just bought some of what you now have for free.

Today my small strong friend and I went back, taking a Japanese carving knife to dig out one of the naked lady bulbs stuck under a root of the tree. It took a long time while Lindy kept watch, being not so sure that the house is actually empty, even though we'd knocked on doors and windows. I felt like a dentist faced with a broken impacted back tooth to be removed. It came out, an immense thing, and now it is planted and the line outside the fence is almost complete. Then Lindy dug out some stinking lilies.

Speaking of fitness, I counted this afternoon and realised that I have four friends now who cannot walk around the block or, if they can, only slowly and no further than that. I keep thinking about Montaigne wanting death to come when he is weeding among his cabbages. Sometimes, when I bend to pick tomatoes my head spins and I don't mean metaphorically. I wonder, because once I fell over, if this is my intimation of mortality or even a happy hint of how I might go. Believe me, if I do, I will not be unhappy. That is, if I am given time to consider it as I lie there with my face in the leaves or gravel, a tomato squashed, perhaps, under my breast. My mother used to say, 'If I die on a Sunday night, don't be sorry, because I will be happy for I will have missed washing day.'

Every woman I know well has a long, obsessive and secret relationship with her kitchen floor. I have just realised this because today, having bought some bizarre slippers, in which the wearer can slide around on floors like Spanish maids using cloths to clean and polish the wooden floors of mansions and hotels as they go, I can now clean as I walk. These strange things look like seaweed and have micro-fibre tassels on their soles to gather dirt and to polish. Few things I ever wear give me more pleasure.

I developed a fetish for cleaning the kitchen floor in the first house Richard and I owned. I'd chosen black and white tiling for all three rooms at the back of the house. Not being experienced, I had no idea of the work that would be involved in cleaning floors marked by two small children and a wheelchair. My children can still picture me walking around on towels, drying off the floors after washing them. These simple tasks can take a grip.

Now, if you will excuse me, I must slide off to ensure there is not a skerrick of dust to be seen.

CABBAGE

A green rose
you lie composed,
quiet and closed as a tomb.

Soon I will take
my biggest silver knife
and quarter you with a crunch,
as a medieval executioner
treated a traitor.

These blows done,
your destiny commences,
butter, bacon, caraway
cream, pork, apple.

Yes, you the edible rose
agree like a famous courtesan
to join any of these, your regulars.

Your name is linked with kings.
Of all those old democrats,
vegetables,
you are the most democratic.

It is of utterly no interest
to you
who takes the knife, the fork—
all gullets being the same—
as you like us
pass into history.

Monday, 15 March

A glorious day at the Garden Expo, although not one of my friends who are gardeners was well enough to come with me today. Is this what old age will be? Lindy, the fit one, was busy.

Bulbs just implore you to buy them. More than almost any other plant, I buy them no matter that I have sworn not to have soft things like bulbs in this rough dry garden.

Geums were on sale and though I have never seen them growing I wanted some because I have read about them in *Gardens Illustrated*.

The money had run out.

I see now that the range of salvias is enormous and because they are hardy, and bring bees, I bought some more pale blue 'African Skies'.

The famous Dutch landscaper Piet Oudolf, who makes gardens in the USA and Europe, used a waving blue flower in a vast mass in a garden he made and I have always longed to have that plant. I discovered today that I already have it. It is called *Perovskia* 'Blue Spire', or Russian sage. I seem to have two kinds, one with a green leaf and a mid-blue flower and another with a more silvery leaf and a darker blue flower. Other than that, they seem to be the same plant. I was electrified to find this for sale. Using my Mastercard to lean on, I borrowed a pen from a woman to write the name down.

She was buying an *Ornithogalum* bulb, which I learnt then and there is what I brought home in a pot thrown out in the street about a year ago. That pot was packed with big pale green bulbs rising up in waves. Today the tag on the bulb for sale said that it needs to be planted with most of the bulb above the ground; and that, because it was hard to dig deeply enough, was how they went in here and now they are flowering with their long fronds of white and green starry flowers up the stem.

Sophie Thomson, the horticulturalist, was on stage talking about organic gardening. She said that if you spray aphids you may be killing ladybirds' eggs which are laid among the aphids to eat them when they hatch. And also, there is a wasp which lays its egg inside the aphid so that its young can eat the aphid when it hatches. I haven't seen a ladybird for years and that, Sophie said, is because we have killed them with insecticides.

I heard that you should remove the lateral branches on pumpkins, cucumbers and zucchini so that the calories go into the fruit. In the morning I am going out to tear down the pumpkin which has almost covered the biggest of the plum trees.

Coming home, I rushed straight to the front with six bearded iris and fifteen 'Erlicheer' daffodils, dug up more of the lawn, and put them in. Certainly iris are rhizomes, not bulbs, but they have the same effect on me.

I have decided to make a memory garden for my daughter. She is so far away. These tough old daffodils are her favourite flower. They grow wild in paddocks. For years I misread their name and called them 'Ericleer', not knowing that their name described them as the first to bloom. In Sydney, I used to buy the flowers for her when I visited her and sometimes had enough in my garden to pick her a bunch.

What a wonderful day. It is rarely that you can go out and come home having learnt things so pleasant to know.

Tuesday, 16 March

Lindy came this morning and sat in the back garden. She says it's been a terrible year for mould on zucchini and pumpkins as there have been fewer bees. I showed her some oriental liliums which came in the box of bulbs from Tesselaars and we saw they were sprouting. They are now in the ground under the persimmon tree and I have made an obstacle area of netting and sticks to save them from the chooks.

Those merry days of rollicking around the front garden are over for the chooks. They may take petunias, silverbeet and capsicum but if they took one of these lovelies I'd be upset and it would be my own fault as I love to let them out. Like the prisoners in *Fidelio*, they rush to freedom and it lifts my heart to see them . . . But like forgetting the hose has been left on, I forget they are out and after a while of fluffing their feathers in a dirt bath, they stand up, shake themselves off and go out to explore. It helps to have something to feed and to care for and they make a sweet sound in the morning.

Thursday, 25 March

Plenty of rain. The wettest summer for many years. A friend, Tim, and his wife, Lea, have been staying with me. He's been my agent for thirty years. For three nights we stayed at an old homestead called 'Murella' looking over the Coorong near the mouth of the River Murray. Tucker has set it up as a conservation reserve. Ti-tree is in blossom so for miles the trees were covered in a creamy froth which brings the bees. They had swarmed on the back verandah and had been poisoned the day we arrived. We could smell the poison. On several other occasions bees have swarmed inside that house and been sent packing. Weird, isn't it? I mean, if you look at a jar of honey and realise that the creature which made that has the power to force a house to be burnt down.

My sister-in-law Patricia gave me 3 litres of honey from the hives kept by the apiarist where she and Tucker live. We had dinner there on Sunday night. Deer were in the paddocks with stags lifting their questions to the sky in silhouette.

'Samba deer are the cleverest of all deer,' my brother said. 'If they don't want you to see them, you won't be able to spot them no matter how hard you look. A samba will hide behind a tree trunk, moving around the trunk as you drive past.'

A few minutes later, as we passed a drain full of tall grasses, I could not see a samba doe, licking her lips with a beautiful pink tongue, which was standing about 2 metres from the car window, until Tucker pointed her out.

Today I pulled out the three largest tomato bushes because they take up space and have only a few green fruit left on them. Cabbages need the space where those bushes were. And I must have a space to fall in when death comes, as Montaigne might say. Perhaps by saying such things I am trying to delay death. Nowadays I want to live to be a hundred but I may change my mind. Jane told me years ago that she knows that she will die at seventy-six. I thought it was a dangerous thing to think as the mind has its sly ways. Next year she will be that age.

Almost every day I count the things I have done. The aim is to have accomplished ten things. Pitiful to admit, but I want to have made some mark. To have achieved something. Even if it is only cleaning a cupboard. Barry Oakley writing in the *Australian Literary Review* about Jane Miller's book *Crazy Age* said that on some days all he accomplishes is a walk to the village. (And I gather the village isn't exactly 20 kilometres away.) Perhaps many people feel the same way.

I've heard that the writer Murray Bail aims for 200 words daily and after that, does he count washing his socks? Or making dinner? What would Louis Nowra count? He said of me that I 'fetishised domesticity'. Too right I do, Louis! Try living without it.

We have colonized a hostile planet, and we must stanch every opening where cold and dark might pour through and destroy the false climates we make, the tiny simulations of forgotten seasons beside the Euphrates, or in Eden. At a certain level housekeeping is a regime of small kindnesses, which, taken together, make the world salubrious, savory, and warm. I think of the acts of comfort offered and received within a household as precisely sacramental. (Marilynne Robinson, *When I Was a Child I Read Books*, Farrar, Straus and Giroux, 2012)

Jane Miller says in her book that by the time she has swum laps in the local pool and translated a page of *Anna Karenina*, the day is almost over. I can never understand how a person can go to bed at night and leave the house tidy enough, most work done and yet next morning there are still dozens of things which need to be done. It is one of the great puzzles of life.

'Now I lay me down to sleep, I pray the Lord my soul to keep and a clean house in the morning.'

Day after day we wonder when the season will break. A dry garden can be a dirty garden, I read in *Gardening Australia* magazine. When I say I am making a dry garden, I do not mean one that has no extra water poured on. I mean one that has plants that can withstand a certain amount of dryness. Many of the trees I have planted need water, some so much that I would not have put them in had I known.

The astrophysicist Professor Brian Cox said on ABC television: 'The Atacama desert is twenty times drier than the Sahara. There are rocks here that have not seen water for twenty million years.' Yet, even there I saw a red-flowering plant along the roadside. People got out of the bus to photograph it. At the mud-brick resort there, irrigated gardens of lucerne were flowering. Everywhere, it seems, people make gardens.

There was nothing unusual about dryness at Tumby Bay where my brothers and I grew up. Yet there was enough water to grow pepper trees, quandongs and wattle. Geraldton wax bushes, Shirley poppies and tomatoes grew from the bowls of washing-up water tossed on them.

Tuesday, 30 March

Beautiful grey pumpkins are falling from the trees. I had no idea how a fresh pumpkin would taste. Along with potatoes, newly dug, it is an utterly delicious vegetable. Especially good when curried with coconut cream or any way at all.

The seeds of the first pumpkin I cut are drying in the sun on top of a bin and as I walked past them this afternoon I wished that I could send a seed of this glorious pumpkin to everybody reading these lines. I believe you could grow a pumpkin in a pot (when the plant is pulled out, it has a surprisingly small root map). It just needs a place to crawl. I'd let it grow over my bed if I had nowhere better.

Strange to see that something so rich and good has come from the garden without me doing a single thing to help it to grow. Yet I have watched the tomatoes like a jeweller and poured on them tomato dust, fertiliser, water, Seasol and every care. I am about to eat both the pumpkin (in a chicken curry) and a raw tomato on the side. Yesterday I cleared out the chook pen, all the old straw and manure, and put two barrow loads of it onto the citrus trees. I love this loop. Feed the birds, and they feed the garden which feeds me.

Plus eggs. Still six daily from six hens. They must like things here. At dusk they become frantic as it is the time I have often let them out into the garden where they are now. I remember a polar bear walking up and down inside the wire of its cage at the Adelaide zoo, half-mad, I suppose, and these birds do the same. So no matter what mess they make, hurling mulch behind them with their long claws, I let them out and watch them stream and scramble to the apricot tree. It is the first tree that they come to and then they scratch like mad, miners knowing gold is an inch away.

I go indoors and watch until they have found a spot where they dig down on the side of the house where I never water, and there all six lie together in a flurry of throwing the soil into their feathers in a joyous silent uproar. They look like a split pillow. Sooner or later they amble out and then they go into the street and the front garden and the damage begins. I run out in whatever I am wearing because I have forgotten they were out and shoo them back to their pen where they go as mildly as school children to a drum.

Wednesday, 31 March

Friends have brought me Gawler sweet peas and dwarf French ones from the Vilmorin company. It says on the packet, among five other languages, 'Dwarf variety giving many butterfly shaped flowers with a delicate scent.' Then from Paula and David from Mornington in Victoria came some from last year's crop, along with Mr Fothergill's 'Mammoth Mix' which it says are 'Early flowering, sweet scented. Ideal for cutting, having long stems.' Then there are the Goodman seeds from Bairnsdale. It says on the packet that only fertilisers containing phosphorous and potash, but no nitrogen, must be used during the growing period. It also says that lime should be added to the soil before planting and compost dug in.

Now the thing is, how to get them to sprout? Lindy has soaked her seeds and they have sprouted. But nobody else suggests that. David says they have had success with laying the seeds between pieces of damp paper towel then leaving them on a windowsill, all the while keeping them damp but not too wet.

The upshot of this is that I have four types of seeds in the laundry on plates covered with damp paper. Last year's seeds from my garden have been sown straight into the bed; quite deeply, as Sophie Thomson from *Gardening Australia* says mice eat them if the seeds are not planted in that way.

SWEET PEAS

Lots of them today
Blooming against the fence
Offering their lilac, purple, magenta and pink clouds
Of scent. Also the floral skirt I bought today
Lying on the bed in its tissues like a tiger.
All these frivolous things
While serious matters are awry.

The air here is full of the flowers' perfume
Even though rain is just a memory
Yet, a vast rainbow appeared over the rooftops.
Sweet peas mean summer's almost here
And this arrhythmia makes me grateful
As my slow pulse blooms like sweet peas
On the fence of my wrist with glorious irregularity
Boom, boom . . . . . . boom.

As you can see, I am keen on these mild horticultural puzzles. They are intriguing and I am willing to spend a lot of time investigating them. Yet I remember a lawn, a trimmed pine tree and a row of gerberas in a neighbour's front garden at Woonona which every year had a north-facing, wire arrangement which was covered in sensational sweet peas. So much among so little. What was his secret, that wild old shouter?

Thursday, 1 April

This morning, on the local bus, sitting beside a woman who said she was ninety-two, I heard her story after I said that a man nearby us was deaf. She said, 'So am I, but I paid $8000 for hearing aids years ago and I don't wear them because I can't stand them.'

I said, 'Did you know that the science is now in and my audiologist told me recently that what they suspected has now been found to be true? Hearing loss that is neglected can lead to dementia? You know, you could go back and have your hearing aids readjusted.'

'Oh, they keep sending me notices but I take no notice. It will just cost me more. My husband was in the British army. He went to . . . oh, what was it called with all the boats?'

'Dunkirk?'

'Yes, that's it. But I don't get a pension because even though I've lived here for all these years, I don't have a Gold Card. Yet, my friend whose husband spent the whole of the war in Alice Springs—Yes, Alice Springs! The whole war!—has a Gold Card. She said she kept on asking for one and she thinks she just wore them down!'

'You could try that, too, perhaps.'

'No, I'm too proud.'

Then she went on: 'I lost three members of my family to the war. My cousin was a gunner and he got shot down. My brother was on the Burma Railway. Have you heard of that?'

'Of course.'

'Well, he came home and he was as thin as that,' holding up her forefinger. 'He only lived two months.'

I asked if she'd had a nice Easter. 'Oh, I didn't see anyone for five days. My family went away—they asked me to come, but I said I couldn't. I used to ride a bike until I was seventy but I was found unconscious on Brighton Road. I had a brain tumour. So I don't ride anymore. I have no trouble keeping busy. My mother was a tailor, she made overcoats during the war for her children from men's jackets. I sew, too, and I take up all my trousers. My legs are so short, you see.'

'You see that woman getting off?' I said. 'She said something striking to me one day, "I am going inside now to face four brick walls." But look, her house has all the curtains drawn and the outside blinds are down. It is always like that. She could see these trees if she opened it up. It bothers me to think of her there in the darkness.'

'Oh,' she said, 'I love the light! I keep all the blinds and curtains open. I see and hear the birds. Little honeyeaters come. Did you know that if you play music to them, they will stay?'

I didn't know that and asked what sort of music she played to the birds. 'Oh, some of my CDs; Chopin. They like waltzes, too.'

Saying that my bus stop was coming up, I stood and said goodbye. Full of respect, realising that I had just heard a short history of the second half of the twentieth century in the West . . .

Thursday, 22 April

Dawn is silver lately and the days cooler. Yesterday I planted purple carrot seedlings and blue pansy seeds. I've been picking persimmons, pumpkins, quinces. Only two of the latter but then the tree was only planted a year ago and is already up to the guttering on Nora's house. It says in *Earth Garden* magazine that pumpkins should be cured if you intend to use them through winter. To cure them, they should be left in the sun for five days and then stored somewhere dry. So that is what I did and now the laundry holds six 'Queensland Blues'.

Today my brother Peter told me, when we were discussing hormone-free beef which is being advertised, that hormones have not been used on poultry for decades. Yet often there are signs in shops advertising hormone-free poultry. He said that when our parents used hormones on roosters, a capsule was inserted in the back of the neck of each bird. The bird would then grow immensely fast and fat. The hormone was so effective that our mother used to put eggs under a rooster and it would sit and hatch chickens. It made me laugh to hear of it.

Never one to waste an opportunity for a bit of frugality, our mother would have been keeping a hen from being broody and thus it would go back to laying while the rooster, which had nothing to do except fertilise eggs and crow, was put to good use. To stop a hen being broody, she would throw a bucket of water over it. 'Necessity is the mother of invention' was one of her favourite sayings, along with 'A little help is worth a ton of sympathy'.

I have been in Sydney where the gutters are full of frangipani flowers and the paths littered with them. At Singleton in the Hunter

Valley I stayed at a winery and every day I walked among the vines and chewed the husks of grapes the pickers left. They were so sweet they tasted like cranberries. There had been such rain that the chardonnay grapes were not harvested because of mould. But the red grapes were picked and will make good wine, the manager said.

I was there to teach memoir writing to senior citizens in the town and I watched carefully because this is my age group and I want to know into what I am heading, even though I have a pretty fair idea. Ardent and free as they may never have been before, they came to class after class. And would be coming yet if they could. People in the country are often hungry for books and for talk about books.

By chance, I had met one of the students on the train coming into the town and as she sat beside me she gave a wonderful monologue of her life, hopping from topic to topic like a happy bird. A gardener, who has made a rockery at her retirement village in a spot of derelict, weedy land about 3 metres square. Or, as she put it, 'From those seats there, to those over there,' gesturing to seats in front and waving across the aisle and back to where we sat. I had never heard the size of a garden described using seating. Noela was her name.

Friday, 21 May

It is a matter of trust. You have to think that somebody trusts you. If you don't believe that, you become paralysed. In an interview in *The Paris Review* Joan Didion was asked what it was that let her feel she could write about intellectual matters for the editor of *The New York Review of Books*, Robert Silvers.

She answered: 'His trust. Nothing else. I couldn't even have imagined it if he hadn't responded.'

I go on with this possibly weird garden, love it though I do but with a sliver of trust.

A woman I had never seen before walked past last week when I was watering in the front garden and told me the garden makes her feel happy when she passes it. 'My name is Dawn,' she said and went on her way.

Buoyed by this stranger's remark, I tore into the browning cannas and lopped them back hard, then dug out a metre or two of couch grass where I wanted to plant vegetables. I have put in four beetroot seedlings which came from the seed box and lots of Shirley poppy seedlings from seeds I bought at the Sydney Botanical Gardens months ago.

It came to me, a few years ago, that true faith has doubt riddled through it. Why I thought this, I cannot say, but I believe it. If you don't doubt, it's not faith, it's just conviction. Conviction lacks the grace that faith has.

The self-sown 'Queensland Blue' pumpkins are resting in the laundry. When a man came to clean the windows, I bartered a pumpkin, some limes from my tree and a jar of quince jam from the new quince tree. When the window cleaner, Danny, who is Dutch, said that cleaning a mirror to the ceiling would cost extra, I said I had no more money but perhaps he would accept barter. No, he said, he did not barter. Then when I showed him what I had to offer, he agreed and now the mirror is immaculate and so are the windows. I could walk through the one which opens out onto the back garden. It is almost invisible.

I did once walk into a window in Kampala when the hotel had a fire alarm going off and I was rushing with my typewriter and manuscript through a cocktail party. Richard Leakey, the famous zoologist, was at a conference for international zoologists. The people seemed indifferent to the sound of the alarm. I shouted that the hotel was on fire but they ignored me. Leaving them to their fate, I ran downstairs and straight into the foyer's plate-glass window. Then a receptionist told me that it was only a test and there was no fire at all. And yet I could smell smoke. I went back to my room, put on the white paste face mask I had removed and lay down and cursed Africa, Uganda, myself and the phoney alarm.

Thursday, 27 May

Now I know why British gardeners have such a range of wet-weather gear and why they work in the rain. I have been out planting poppy seedlings in the rain. Exhilarated, I then put in thirty-eight bulbs among the belladonna lilies along the side fence. My friend Tarla brought me these bulbs in a paper bag weeks ago, saying she had dug them up from a hillside at Quorn where she lives and that they are crinum lilies. But these are nothing like the description in *Botanica*. I mislaid the bag and when I found them they had sprouted.

As I planted the poppies, I harvested half a dozen leeks which were planted nearly a year ago. Somewhere I read that leeks take a long time to grow and these are small even after all that time. Eggplant are everywhere, front and side, lolling over with the weight of their leaves but, again, small fruit. Last year a different type, perhaps, had huge fruit and a lot less foliage. It may be that they have had too much chicken manure and the energy went into the leaves. Nonetheless, this morning I fried four with the leeks and tomatoes and cumin.

Winter

Tuesday, 8 June

In an effort to have more time I have hired a cleaner. It took some doing. One man had advertised in the local paper with a list of what he would do, including dusting. For some reason this appealed to me: imagine a cleaner refusing to dust! However, on three occasions he could not come, so on the third mishap, I didn't ring back. But, like dealing with a council, the great thing is perseverance. 'The squeaking wheel gathers the oil' my neighbour once said to me and it took me a while to figure it out. I have found it to be true. Any council I have ever contacted has, in the end, been obliging.

Then, remembering Jane's cleaner, Lyn, I rang her. She agreed to come. On the day she was meant to work, she became lost in Glenelg and, though I rode out on my bike to look for her, we both gave up after an hour and each went back to our homes. Then, with perseverance and a map, Lyn came last Monday. She spent two hours on the fridge. A fanatic about use-by dates, she began to throw things out. In fact, I realised that there was nothing in the fridge, except wine, that was not past its use-by date. I persuaded her to let me have a few things to eat, but the rest went in the bin. It now looks like an operating theatre. Stainless steel and glass gleaming, flooded with light shining on a few jars. My friend Louise said I should have taken before and after photos.

One summer's day when Louise was twenty-four and had brown wavy hair to her waist, she was sleeping late, wearing a long white Victorian cotton nightdress. While she slept, the young man she had stayed with rose, then dressed in a waiter's uniform of white shirt, black tie, black waistcoat and jacket.

After a while, Louise heard a recording of Mahler's 5th Symphony being played so she went to investigate. In the back garden of the young man's house, a goat was tethered and hens ran around. Men were at work at a construction site next door. The man had set up a table covered with a white cloth and a single chair among the tall grass. He invited her to sit.

While the music played, Louise was served a two-course lunch with wine. For the entire time it took her to eat the meal, the man stood and waited on her but did not speak.

The workmen came out, opened their lunch boxes and, observing the scene, began to cheer. Still no word from the man, but when the food was eaten and the wine drunk, he pulled out her chair, took Louise's hand and led her to the bed.

She told me this story years ago and I believe it.

The bathroom, which had deliberately been cleaned before Lyn came, took her an hour. She sent me out to buy bleach before I could show her Shannon Lush's book *Spotless*, which recommends bicarbonate of soda and white vinegar for cleaning almost anything. This mixture could nearly fix a broken heart.

Thursday, 8 July

Storms for two days. Drab, wild storms with heavy rain. Since I came back two weeks ago from the Watermark Literary Muster (which the late Eric Rolls began at Kendall, near Port Macquarie) we have had four or five inches of rain. I forget the exact number, because when tipping out the overflowing rain gauge I lost count.

In the shed there are six point-of-lay pullets which Peter bought for me while I was away. He left them locked in the shed, separated from the six red hens in the open run. This is because the red ones defend their territory fiercely. Even though I had chosen the same number of new hens, I had to have white ones as there were no red available. Though the white are bigger than the red, when a red hen gets into the shed white feathers fly and the new ones rush to the nesting cupboard and crush in there, becoming so limp I thought one was dead.

It has turned into the War of the Roses. So now the red ones are out of their shed under umbrellas; which is how this business of having chooks began. They now sleep on straw in the dog kennel which was their first home. Annabel painted in gold script above the kennel doorway 'Bless this Nest' when she gave me the kennel.

The new plan is to allow the white hens to become so accustomed to the shed that when the red hens are let in, they will put up a fight and soon things will settle. It could all be theirs, red and white, if only they would share.

Now home from a walk to lunch at a bistro with Joanie, I remember that Colette said a woman should never leave home unless dressed as if to meet a lover. We ran into an old boyfriend of mine on Brighton Jetty and as we walked away after a chat I began to cough.

I remembered being with him at Clare in March when the mouldy vines gave the grapes the noble rot and gave me asthma.

LOVEMAKING WITH ASTHMA

If you lower your shoulder
one inch more
I'm a dead woman.

A flock of birds
has landed in my lungs
their cries come from my mouth
their feathers fill my throat
my lungs' branches creak.

As the heart pumps
its old rhythms and desires,
these lisps and drums
of the lungs
sigh like sirens
combing their hair
in such warm air
to lure you
in the heart's calamitous rocks.

I have been explaining to my son why I think that the sight of many elderly frail people in a dining room in a hospital or in an aged care home, though at first harrowing, would be less alarming or disturbing if those people now at the end of their lives were seen as at the beginning. Seeing them sitting at a table wearing a bib, being fed, and not altogether aware of what is going on, could then be charming and not at all alarming or horrific. I tell him this so that if he sees me in such a condition he will be able to bear it by turning me in his mind into a three-year-old.

The consolation of the garden is now even deeper, if that is possible. Probably not, but it feels wonderful to see that the mandarins are ripe, about thirty of them on one tree, and limes are falling from their tree. The two buckets of olives from the trees in the front garden are curing in the laundry and there are figs from the garden in syrup in the cupboard. So all is not lost. And how these dozen hens keep my spirits up. There is nothing like caring for something to help to keep a feeling of worth. Even the heaviest yoke can be lifted.

The good, even delightful, news is that I have befriended Nora next door. It only took two dozen eggs. Tomatoes which I had left on her door step were never acknowledged, probably because she didn't know where they came from. But I took a dozen eggs and left them on the step and a month later took in some out-of-date crumpets and another dozen eggs and found Nora on her new Zimmer frame walking out towards the path. She smiled happily and I saw how soft her face is, and she said that she was just going out to the letterbox.

I noticed that the strelitzia—to which she had so strenuously objected when I first came here and introduced myself, saying that it had to be burnt or dug out—was again sending out leaves around her letterbox. I said that I would come and clip back the leaves.

Nora shrugged slightly and said, 'Oh! I don't really mind!' Two dozen eggs, that is what it took, and two and a half years.

Friday, 9 July

A willie wagtail comes to the back garden many afternoons. He has landed on a bare branch of the apricot tree and looks like a man in a dinner suit dancing. Twice his normal size, he has puffed himself up because of the cold. Indigenous people call willie wagtails gossip birds because they gather round when people sit down to talk. My friend Diana told me this when we used to go to watch brides at Sandon Point: for years we went on Saturdays, walking by the sea with friends, and then had afternoon tea picnics there.

Here the temperature in the mornings is now between 4 and 5 degrees and the days 15 degrees or less. But it is cosy indoors, as there are big windows facing north and east. When I first came here, until I got shutters, I had to wear a hat when making tea in the kitchen because of the morning sun.

How comforting birds are. They are like dogs. They need no language to make us feel cheerful, they just exist in their own mysterious world which they seem to share with us when we watch them. A new bird has come to the garden. One I've never seen before. At first I thought it was a regent bowerbird but it has different markings, black and grey stripes. It is alone and has been here for three or four days and strides around the garden. Perhaps it blew in on one of the storms. Looking up *The Birds of Australia*, it seems that it could be a spotted nightjar (*Eurostopodus argus*). That, or a sea bird, as its legs are rather long. Or, a painted snipe (*Rostratula benghalensis*). Any of the above, or none. Perhaps you know. Tell me.

Wednesday, 14 July

Last year I discovered that there are secrets to being joyful.

The first happened when Peter Goldsworthy drove me into Writers' Week from his home where I'd stayed after a dinner. I arrived early because he was on his way to work. The British writer Sarah Waters, whom I'd heard speak before, was addressing a packed crowd in one of the two huge tents. She'd written a marvellous book set in the London Blitz and I had bought six copies for friends I liked it so. But I didn't fancy hearing her again, so dragged a chair up to sit in the sun and wait for the next speaker. However, I could still hear. She was riveting because she spoke of how she writes, not on what she writes. About her aims and ambition, which is, after all, what is most interesting to know of any artist. It seemed to me that it was a wonderful thing to be there listening, not to the talk re-broadcast on radio, but with the writer in the flesh, hearing her directly. It was a little epiphany.

I saw that it is good to be present in good places. I mean, to put yourself in an art gallery, a concert hall, a garden, on a jetty, or just by the sea or any other lovely place. I made a little motto, so small it seems trivial. 'Put yourself in good places.' Since that day I have tried to. It is something vaguely related to the Buddhist idea of 'being present'. For example, the saying, 'If you are sweeping the path, sweep the path.'

The second helpful thing was that one day I saw, as in a bolt of lightning, another thing so simple that it seems almost too obvious to mention. It was that it is not what you do in big spurts of energy from time to time, rather, it is the small things you do daily which comprise your life and make it meaningful. For instance, the daily porridge; good for the gut. Kindness, some small thing done to another. The daily walk. A swim. A bike ride. Flowers given to a friend. Avoiding platitudes. Avoiding complaint. Praise coming readily to the lips.

As I sat there casting about for illustrations of what I mean, a friend's letter was on the desk. In it, my friend, John Miller, a psychiatrist in his fifties who used to run half-marathons until a recent diagnosis of terminal cancer, wrote: 'I have discovered the Book Depository on the internet and a book is heading your way. I could have left you guessing, but it felt better to let you know that I can be just as thoughtful for the ageing, as you can be for the dying.'

Yesterday an enormous book arrived called *Fruit*, published by Firefly Books, by P. Blackburne-Maze and lavishly illustrated with Renaissance paintings. I will use it for the rest of my life. I have learnt not to say 'for years' as it may tempt fate. I can remember Robert Holmes à Court being interviewed on television, about his work as Chairman of the Board of the West Australian Art Gallery. When asked of his plans for the future, he said, 'I'll be behind this desk.' Wrong. He died within a year.

Now the third idea I have forgotten. It will have to wait. A perfect illustration of ageing.

It may have been that what you intend to do in the future, do daily. As the Greek hero Milo lifted the bull by lifting the calf daily.

On another matter, Marcus Aurelius wrote: 'Everything is but what your opinion makes it; and that opinion lies with yourself. Renounce it when you will, and at once you have rounded the foreland and all is calm; a tranquil sea, a tideless haven.' (Book X11 number 22.)

Thursday, 29 July

The first bee arrived yesterday. Lately, I think that a well-spent day is one when small things get done.

For instance, today was what I aim for. In bed drinking tea, I wrote a long letter to a friend who has just had a novel published. I fed the chooks a mixture of old bread, water and yoghurt and collected ten eggs.

Waiting at the doctor's surgery I read Sarah Bakewell's book *How to Live: A Life of Montaigne* which I love. The perfect book for this time and it just fell into my hands via a scrap of paper on which I had scrawled the title from a radio interview with the author. Then the library bought it for me. The Marion Library is the best one I have ever used. (They even bought, when I asked, *The Crimea*, a huge book which was expensive and one I don't imagine will have many takers.) Riding off with the prescriptions, I bought pansy seedlings and petunia seeds because the hens have dug up the spring flowers in the pots at the back door.

I see now that I can't let the poultry roam, as I can't protect the plants even though they have wire and deer antlers and olive branches and any sticks of prunings I can find over them. It doesn't work. Those long pale legs are strong and the claws simply rip things. So I have made a chicken run down one side of the house which is cemented and they can come out from their dog kennel and cage for a few hours daily. When the red ones are let out, the white ones come from the shed and can scratch in the cage.

Almost daily I learn things about poultry simply by having them here.

On the way home I called on Lindy who has remade her front garden because in a wind last summer her beautiful grey stone fence was crushed by a native paperbark street tree which blew down. She was enraged because she had asked the council for a jacaranda tree but was told that the arborist said paperbarks were most suitable for the area. Yet every one of those trees in the street blew over. After ten months she has a new fence, not stone, and the insurance company gave her $2000 for the garden to be remade. We walked around with Robert, Lindy's husband, looking at what she has done and admiring it. Now she has a dry garden ready for their old age.

In the back courtyard Robert brought out tea and we sat talking, looking at the limbs of a golden elm tree which is to be pruned to cast less shade on the vegetable garden.

At home I planted seedlings and put seeds into seed boxes. Then lay in the sun in the back room spitting prune stones and missing the dish of yoghurt and raw oats while reading the Montaigne book so avidly I couldn't make myself raise my head for better aim.

Living alone I can do this sort of thing and find no criticism.

Later a man from Croatia came to quote to lay a wooden floor over the old cement one under the dining table and I gave him a dozen eggs to take home to his wife.

Now, all there is to do is to eat this roast turkey leg with vegetables and retire with the book. Is that not a pleasant day? As far as I know, I have harmed nobody, not even myself, and how grateful I am. There were other things I meant to do, such as mowing the lawn and pruning a lot of Mexican sage, but the day is over.

Thursday, 5 August

Peace in our time. At last, the chooks, drenched in rain, have accepted each other. I was thinking how shameful it is that as poultry fight and persecute each other, so do we. 'We are no better than chooks!' I thought a few days ago, after a quarrel with Peter. It will be interesting to see if the older red hens go back into the shed to their old roosts, or if they have forgotten that place and will sleep in the dog kennel where they've been for two months or more.

This seems like a scientific experiment. So, if you introduce hens to those that have been in a shed longer, separation will, in the end, make peace.

Now, if only I could apply this to matters closer to my life.

I am drinking the most terrible wine; it tastes like kerosene. Lyn, who has just cleaned the house, drove me in the rain to buy wine and even though I have had the brand before, this type, new to me, is terrible. And there is nothing in the house but gin or Marsala or Noilly Prat vermouth to drink.

It has rained all day and I have bailed out the big green bin under the overflowing gutter onto fruit trees many times.

The backyard, which has been torn apart by the chooks which are now not let out there, has nothing left but trees and the thrice-planted pots at the back door. I have given up. You can have a garden or you can have chooks but you can't, unless you have a huge piece of land, have both. Peter tried to tell me this but I thought it could be managed. Wrong.

Now there are small white annual daisies under the plum and cuttings of the canes of Peri's tall pink fuchsias. All of these plants have been put in during the last few days.

Saturday, 7 August

It is marvellous what can be achieved after staying in bed until noon. I leapt out thinking that my bed looked like Tracey Emin's and went straight to work. Seeing the damage the chooks have done at the back and how little difference the seedlings and cuttings I put in there yesterday have made, I planted about thirty succulents cut from the front garden. Then I weeded the lawn away from the cumquats' trunks in the front. Because of the rain the chook run is a wet ruin so I cleared it out and tipped the barrow loads of hay and manure onto trees.

I melted down about a litre of cooking fat which was thrown out at the supermarket and soaked two loaves of bread from the same bin in the dripping and gave it to the chooks. The theory behind this is that much related to egg laying depends on calories. Lindy said, 'Oh! They are such greedy birds!' I said, 'If you had to lay a piece of pure protein the size of your head daily, you'd be hungry, too.'

On the matter of the civil war out there, I spoke too soon. The red and white still need to be kept apart for some of the day. There was an outbreak of renewed squawking today, so spoiling things for themselves, the violent red hens have been put back into the kennel and its little yard. This is going to take longer if it is ever to succeed and perhaps it never will. I simply can't bear the way the white hens crouch and freeze in terror when the red ones peck their necks and combs. I read in a book on poultry-keeping that cannibalism can break out, so it is best not to let blood be drawn.

Marvellous what you can get used to. Having left it too late today to return the wine and buy better, I am forced to drink what I have and it is remarkable how acceptable it now is. The wine has either improved with being opened, or I am desperate, or a combination of both. Or, perhaps the first bottle was faulty and the rest not.

More rain due tonight.

Is this not a wonderful life?

Sunday, 8 August

Floods. Out of nowhere came rain so heavy that both the front and back gardens have been flooded. Then hail. I stood looking out wondering how high the water would rise and if it would come over the step. A little bit afraid but exhilarated, too, by the bounty of the water, I ran out in bare feet to look at the rain gauge on the front lawn and the beautiful, cold, clear water rose to my ankles. I could have knelt and lapped it like a dog.

Within a couple of hours, though, the rain stopped and the water subsided. I was thinking of the deep roots of the trees and how well it would prepare them for summer.

Nothing to do except lash on an apron and bake biscuits.

Monday, 9 August

I found orange daylilies forgotten in the front garden. These discoveries are because I am still pruning back the grey plectranthus, lavenders, Mexican sage and the old purple stocks which have grown from seed I gathered from stocks among the rocks by the beach. Last summer these stocks, which have grown to be more like shrubs, tough and lovely, put on such a flowering I wished I owned a camera. Many things have appeared since this pruning began. Dutch iris, for instance, which I planted soon after coming here. Kniphofia, too, which has never flowered but may now that it has been released.

Then I pruned Barbara's white roses across the road because they are tall and full of red hips. She said I might after I explained that if the roses were not cut back she would not have many flowers at Christmas.

There is something deeply satisfying about pruning. It may be a destructive streak in me to hack and slash. Also, one knows that it will make the plant prosper. (There are not many things which one can half destroy and know that it is doing them good.)

Do you know, I talk to you as I garden? I ask myself if you would be interested in this small thing. Having restricted myself to such a narrow palette as nature writing, I keep wondering if you would like to know of this or that.

For instance, two days ago I found that the blood orange (which has been given a less repellent name of orange sanguine recently) has the first buds in three years since its planting. I had rung a radio station gardening advice program to ask why the blood orange has never flowered. The horticulturalist found this amusing and said that, of course, I had probably been feeding it. I said that I had. He then explained that this only leads to more lush growth, as the tree is trying to use all the nitrogen taken in by its roots. It has no chance to pause and make flowers, because if it doesn't make leaves it will die of nitrogen poisoning or something like that. He has seen blood oranges growing in the Middle East on stony ground without much water, but with much sun, thriving. The advice was that I should remove all fertiliser from the tree and then bind a branch tightly with wire to stress and to scarify it to make the tree feel that it is in danger. (Surely, this is a tree feeling and then thinking.)

I raced out, dragged all the mulch placed there (from last year's plants of tomatoes and pumpkins) away from the base, and then bound two big branches with wire and twisted it around and around the bark until flakes fell like dandruff. Enough to put the wind up any tree. This was about a month ago.

Sure enough, as I showed Lindy today, there are barely visible dots of blossom on the tips of several branches. And not just on the ones which have been bound, either. How strange, that neglect and hardship were the answer. I suppose the reason is that the tree has been well fed and watered and not that blood oranges need nothing at all, just not too much of anything.

'Too much of a good thing is wonderful,' is what Peri once embroidered on a cushion. When I stand and look at it, as it lies on the guest's bed at her house, I sniff a bit and rub my face and wonder. Then I lie on it and wonder no longer.

Friday, 13 August

So many sick friends. Today, one came to lunch and I think she won't see the year out. We walked down the street looking at the new houses built where old ones were and it was an effort for her to get even near the end of the street. I was afraid when I saw her. Maybe I will die before her, but it doesn't look that way right now. Lyn the cleaner said, quite innocently because she has recently done a course in domiciliary care, that my friend should be careful not to get bedsores. This caused a bit of grim laughter, between my friend and me, but there was a grain of truth in it.

The latest medical news is that exercise is the new anti-cancer aid. A doctor speaking on radio said that people used to be sent home after cancer treatment and told to rest, and now they are told to exercise. My friend has not been for a walk, except the one we took today, since her dog died two months ago. I said a few weeks ago, 'It's walk or die!' Harsh, maybe, and there are plenty of reasons to 'potter', as she puts it, 'in the garden', but I feel like screaming, 'Walk or die!' I do not want to lose her.

When Lindy comes to walk with me on Monday, I know, thank heaven, she will set off at a cracking pace and go for three hours or more and think nothing of it. But then, Lindy and I are well and my friend is not. But would she be well, if she had been walking for the past five years and not just pausing every few metres for a little dog to investigate a smell by a pole or a tree?

Sometimes I think these things are decided long ago and are part of our personality or our DNA.

Some people like to move, and get cranky if they don't, and some do not like to move much at all.

And on this, perhaps, hang all the laws and the prophets.

Tuesday, 17 August

Spring is close. Many of the scented bulbs are flowering. There are four blue hyacinths growing in pots on a blue-checked dish on the kitchen bench. Also, there's a glass of white hyacinths, cream freesias (which smell, not like old freesias, but of patchouli), 'Erlicheer' and one perfumed, orange-centred, frilled daffodil by my bed. It is new to have a scented daffodil.

There was news yesterday that Kangaroo Island is running out of food. The two ferries which bring people and supplies to the island are out of use for a few days. There is no bread, milk, eggs, meat or vegetables left in the shops. How can this be? This is a fertile island with good rainfall. They've still got plenty of honey, because there are apiarists. But you can't live on honey. For some reason, I find this situation shocking. And the reason that it's shocking lies in the question, 'How can we have become so complacent that we do not plant food in our gardens?' There is a tourist industry on the island, it is true, and lots of holiday shacks and houses. These visiting people all need to be fed. But there are thousands of acres of farmland which could feed everybody. I don't have an answer but I find it shocking. Are migrants the only people who have an experience of war and suffering who still grow some of their food in their gardens?

I am no farmer, but I am a farmer's daughter and I reckon I could last a month on what is here on this block. Maybe I am boasting. I include what is in the cupboards. There are the 'Queensland Blue' pumpkins in the laundry. Eleven eggs were laid today. I could barter eggs. There are lots of mandarins and limes and onions from last year still growing in the garden. There's a meal or two in that, surely. It is the shame of growing nothing when you are well and have land that gets me. And the waste.

Thursday, 19 August

The Kangaroo Island ferry began sailing again today, making six trips carrying food and people. Usually the ferry makes four trips daily. Perhaps I was smug saying that it seems wasteful not to have enough food to keep the people on the island fed for more than a week. It is always interesting to see what makes your blood boil, as these things can have deep roots and hide fears and inadequacies. What is it that I fear? Hunger. And not being able to feed my family or friends.

In India about a decade or two ago, there was suddenly almost no petrol available. The lines of vehicles went on for kilometres and I saw then that a car is completely useless for its normal purpose without fuel. It can only be used as a shed for animals or poultry or, if desperate, you can sleep in it.

One of my friends made a garden in the back of her station wagon in Poole in Dorset and drove it daily to work. The heat in the car helped the pot plants grow and she had flowers blooming in the back that she could not grow in her garden. Schizanthus is what she grew. So pretty, waving there as she drove by.

Yesterday I cooked a duck for a friend's birthday lunch. How a duck can be sold for only $20 when it has been killed, dressed and frozen and then the butcher, who bought it from the breeder, has made a profit, I do not know. My brother Tucker says that food has never been so cheap in the whole of human history. It is a puzzle to me, because I can pay $10 for a fresh, dressed chicken which will feed up to six people and I paid $15 each for the six white point-of-lay pullets recently. Work and care and food went into breeding all this poultry and now, feeding my own, I do not understand how it can be sold so cheaply.

Then yesterday, while three of us ate the duck with an orange and star anise sauce, a Rick Stein recipe, my chooks, all twelve of them, red and white, laid a dozen eggs. I give the eggs away as it is good karma and I never met a person who wasn't glad to have fresh eggs given to them. (Apart from my parish priest and he was merely startled. Never, perhaps, while gowned up outside the church, having experienced that.)

Sunday, 22 August

Have you seen this day? It's windless with a blue sky and riding my bike is like gliding through pure, clean thought. Yesterday I cleaned out the chook pen again and put two barrow loads of hay and manure on the two olive trees in the front garden. Already since their hard pruning they have pale shoots on the end of cut branches. It is from these shoots that the fruit will come. There are now (let me go and count them) ten jars of olives in oil on the kitchen bench. And I gave one jar today to Peter, so two buckets of olives in brine gave eleven jars. They took a long time to be ready as this time I did not cut them to leach out the bitter juice. Nonetheless, having been in buckets in the laundry for several months (with just a change of brine about once or twice a week), they are ready to eat.

I think there must be as many recipes for pickling olives as there are regions in Greece, Italy, Spain and the south of France. One method uses no water, only rock salt and sun. Also, in another recipe, there's a lot of talk about being able to float a fresh egg in the brine in which the olives are to steep. But it takes an enormous amount of salt to get it to that stage and when I did that, the olives had to be soaked in fresh water for weeks afterwards to remove the brine and make them edible. I mention this because when I told people that I was pickling olives, several of them became ardent that I try their recipe even though they understood that the olives were already experiencing mine. And mine is barely a recipe, more a hit-and-miss bit of method which I made up out of laziness.

Speaking of cooking duck, which I was earlier, my sister-in-law

Patricia rang this morning and said that a workman, Mick, had let a freezer beside a shearing shed go off for several days. She had just dressed twenty-two ducks she had reared, and all the ducks and a huge amount of venison in the freezer spoiled and had to be buried. She said, 'I don't know what's got into Mick. He's been going north to help Tom so much, I think he's lost the plot. I just wish those ducks were still walking around their yard.' It seemed a mild thing to say after all her work. But Tucker is busy in the north having a thousand wild horses caught and sent off to abattoirs; while on another property, 20,000 feral goats were rounded up and sent off to the Middle East. So how can a woman make a man feel that a few ducks are important to her when he's been dealing with figures like that?

Monday, 23 August

Today I planted out strawberry runners. These have multiplied from one survivor of those given as a bonus with each fruit tree I bought from Perry's Fruit and Nut Nursery. There are flowers on the strawberry plants and now some are planted down on the western side of the house among the cabbages, the limes, the orange and mandarin trees. I love this bounty.

On our walk on Saturday morning, Lindy and I clawed out, with bare hands, beautiful deep orange almost burgundy gazanias from a deserted house and garden on the esplanade. Now they are in the front garden replacing the yellow gazanias we got from the same garden and which have spread widely in among the irises. I don't want yellow, it's orange I'm after. (When we got the first lot, they could not have been in bloom.)

Another joyful discovery. Hidden among the yellow gazanias, the white and the blue irises are in heavy bud. I had read in the local paper that the flat grey leaves ought to be cut back so that the plants give more energy to flowering. On reading this, two months ago, I did that and here is the result. I scraped off as much earth as I could to expose a bit of the rhizome of each iris, because if the sun hits it, it is more likely to bloom. So roll on sun.

Wednesday, 25 August

Dolphins galore. Just as Lindy said, 'I don't think there are any dolphins today,' I saw a white splash and there they were. One, then two and then, perhaps, a dozen. Two began to dance, throwing their tails in the air. Their bodies white in the sun. I hugged Lindy's thin shoulders and we stood, off and on, during the walk watching the dolphins as they went north then south. They may have been herding a school of fish.

There is something joyful about seeing dolphins and I have heard that when depressed people swim among them they are less unhappy. In the last few days since warm weather has come, we have been looking for dolphins as they seem to come when the sea is calm. It may only be that they are more visible then.

Now here is another pleasant surprise. When I drank tea in Lindy's garden a few weeks ago, I saw a small pile of sticks lying on the pavement by a tap. I asked if I could have the cuttings as I saw that they were the prunings of her superb tree of apricot-coloured angels' trumpets (*Brugmansia* species). Now, outside my western fence, where there's a line of naked ladies, a row of the cuttings have a leaf or two. We noticed them as we set off on the walk. All they need now is water for their first summer.

Nora's son Joe has come to live with her next door. As he drove his van past two nights ago when I was raking up plectranthus branches in the dusk, he stopped and asked me if I would like another hen. I said that I would. He told me it is black and about eighteen months old, and is free because the owners do not want it. Now, France can join in with the War of the Roses. This is the man who had offered to help his mother by burning down my strelitzia. See, the healing art of eggs.

Thursday, 26 August

That bird hiding in the thicket in the front garden is a rail, I think. A Lewin's rail. Today, I cleaned one of the two flattish water bowls and refilled it. A few hours later, at one o'clock in the afternoon, the bird came again and again to the water and washed itself ecstatically. It ran away, leaving only the light trembling on the water. Then it returned and began again. It takes little notice of trains or cars or other birds, but the moment it sees a person it runs across the lawn and hides. (There is another type of rail, the buff-banded rail, but it is bigger than this one which has a white eyebrow and a russet nape.)

Standing on my lawn three days ago, I was talking with Roland, who comes daily to garden at his empty house opposite, when his mother arrived. I introduced myself and she said her name is Romaine. The bird appeared, splashing in a more sheltered bowl than the one in the sun where it washed today, and I asked Roland if he knew its name. He had not seen it but said that his mother was the bird expert but she had only glimpsed it. After this little vignette Romaine invited me to call in and to see her garden which is nearby and has frogs and a great rose arbour. It is so beautiful that Lindy took Robert there last summer to show him. So I may have made a friend.

Tuesday, 31 August

The black hen came two nights ago. She was in a sealed box, sleeping in a shopping bag. Joe handed it over and when I asked him to let her out into the laundry he shuddered and said that he could not. Jackie French, writing in my favourite magazine *Earth Garden*, said that poultry sleep surprisingly deeply. It is true. The hen could barely be roused to tip her out of the bag. Next morning, alert and ready for anything, she went into the pen of white hens and took no notice of them, nor did they take any of her. It is as if the French queen has come and no creature dare disturb her.

As I was gathering eggs, a red hen squeezed through the gate separating red and white and was soon routed by the new arrival. How quickly the red fled. A bully met her match. How easily a bully cowers once confronted. I wish I could learn this and apply it. But mainly, I am the cowering kind and a bully takes one look and seems to know it. I rarely stand my ground, I simply flee. I lost a wonderful pink silk antique shawl that way. I left it at a man's house, fled and never went back. Then, to cement my fondness for this black hen, she laid a brown egg on the first morning. Talk about calm.

On Sunday, I had a rush of seed sowing. Zinnias, purple climbing French beans, cornflowers, cucumbers, Californian poppies, sunflowers and basil; all those seeds were sown straight onto the ground. Last year I tried to transplant zinnia seedlings and only three plants survived. The label says to sow into the ground and now I have learnt. 'The hard way' as my mother would say. Slugs have eaten all the sprouting seeds in the seed boxes because I left the boxes sitting on a path. I ask myself, when will I ever learn?

The base of the seed boxes sheltered slugs lying there, sly as lies. Now those two seed boxes and two new ones are up on the back table and full of beetroot, orange cosmos (from the gigantic plant which grew over 2 metres high last year) and tomato seeds. No more of these 'Roma' and other tomatoes. Last year none were much good. I have 'Grosse Lisse' because they have been most fruitful. Perhaps there will never be a harvest like the one in the first year when Claudia saw the size of the crop, abandoned the bucket I gave her to collect tomatoes and fetched the wheelbarrow. Perhaps it was the virginity of the soil. It was like a dream. The ardent child, the opulence of the red, red crop, the barrow half full and nothing spoilt by fruit fly. No spray or poison used. How I bless our quarantine and the way it has kept fruit fly out.

The beautiful visiting bird is out morning and evening. It is like a guest, most welcome and mysterious. Will it stay? Why did it come? Where did it come from? When I open the front door it runs into the aloes from the bowl where it was splashing. Sometimes out there, I see a shadow move as I pull a weed or two, or pick up the paper. I look away and pretend I have seen nothing. Then I slink inside, stand at the window and watch the bird emerge. It has a white eyebrow. And I, myself, am growing one.

Today twenty-five 'White Dragon' Christmas lilies were planted beneath the 'Mariposa' plum and the fig tree at the back door. Only four of those same bulbs, which bloomed so well in the first year, have survived the chooks scratching. They were traded, for eggs.

Now, however, I am sterner, and a barrier of wire and bins is set in place so that when the red hens are let out, they have a puzzle to solve. They solve it sometimes but strangely, they have learnt to stay close by and now never go out scratching in the pots near the back door or down into the side vegetable garden or anywhere really destructive. It is as if they have comprehended what is acceptable. They have traded a spot to flush their wings with soil under the small blood plum for the wild range they once had. We have reached a peaceful state.

Speaking of figs, here is a poem that uses them.

BREASTS

As I lean over to write
one of my breasts warm as a breast from the sun
hangs over as if to read what I'm writing
these breasts always want to know everything
sometimes exploring the inside curve of my elbow
sometimes measuring a man's hand
lying still as a pond
until he cannot feel he is holding anything
but water
then he dreams he is floating

in the morning my breast is refreshed
and wants to know something new
although it is soft it is also ambitious
we never speak
but I know my breast knows me more than I do

prying hanging over fences
observant as a neighbour
or eager as a woman wanting to gossip
they tell me nothing
but they say quite a lot about me

there is a dark blue river vein here
straggling down taking its time
to the little pale strawberry
picked too soon and left too long
in the punnet in a warm shop

when I lie
these breasts spread like spilt milk
and standing naked in the sea
float like figs
as you will realise
these are my body's curious fruit
wanting to know everything
always getting there first
strange as white beetroot
exotic as unicorns
useless as an out of order dishwasher
more of a nuisance than anything else

some men seem to think highly of them
peering and staring
what they don't know is
the breast stares straight back

Winter

interested as a reporter

some love them
and invest them with glamour
but like life they are not glamorous
merely dangerous

Spring

Sunday, 5 September

It is spring and the air knows it. As I rode out today, it was like gliding through honey. The plum tree has white blossom. The apricot, pink. Citrus is weighed down with blossom and, like a miracle, even the blood orange has thousands of pale buds. It was the removal of mulch and the denial of food, along with the scarring of two branches with wire, that has made it bloom. For as long as we both lived, the tree and I would have gone on neither pleasing the other if it were not for the gardener on the radio who told me what to do.

Wattle has been blooming along the railway line for weeks and I heard, also on the radio, that it is the pollen of this flower, which holds no nectar, that the bees use to tide the hive over until real nectar arrives with the spring flowering of the trees and plants.

The first blowflies have come. I am a swatter. Also, now there is a sticky coil of tape on sale which was used years ago to hang, usually in the kitchen and dairies, as a trap for flies and it is back on the market. I am not sure if guests here find it repellent, but I have hung two and I think that they are better than spray because they are harmless, even to babies.

The rail is not, as I had thought, a flightless bird. I discovered this when I walked down to the chook pen and found it there trapped by my presence with no escape. Retreating, I stood a while at the back door, but it saw me as it was retreating from the cul-de-sac so it rushed back to the fence of the pen. I gave up and walked quietly down to gather eggs. It suddenly took flight and flew straight over the chook shed into the front garden where it normally lives.

Today I rang *Australia All Over* to see if a listener could identify this bird. Is it a buff-banded rail or a Lewin's rail or some other bird entirely? I think it has a white eyebrow but, if so, it is much smaller than a buff-banded rail which has a white eyebrow and which is about 30 centimetres tall. Perhaps this is a juvenile, sent out of the nest to make its own way. It is welcome here and it was my luck that it came. I never could afford an upright birdbath, even though they keep birds safe from cats. And now I am glad, because I think this bird would not have come if there were not the two flat bowls of water near the thick greenery in which it hides. It only flies when it must. It does not enjoy it, in my opinion.

Wednesday, 8 September

Peonies and hippeastrums. Ever since Lindy's beautiful, hand-built front stone wall was knocked down by a falling tree, she has been wanting to make a new garden with peonies in it. It has been difficult to buy them. But today, at the Royal Agricultural Show, she found them thrown out at a sale.

I have wanted to grow hippeastrums since I saw Peri's huge pots of red flowers at Christmastime about a decade ago. I gasped at the sight. They were so like her. 'She's a ruby sort of woman, isn't she?' her husband Bob said wistfully to me when we were discussing what he might buy her for their ruby wedding anniversary. And, being one quarter Chinese, she wears a lot of red, so these flowers suit her. Extravagantly lovely, a plant of high style; hers were raging red.

I love the way at events such as these, that when handling a few bulbs in a quizzical way, a person standing beside you will suddenly advise you. An elderly man who had a handful of the bulbs himself said, pointing to the 'Apple Blossom' hippeastrums I was poking among, 'Those are the toughest of them all.' Then he pointed to a green point among several other green points on a bulb and said, 'That is the flower.' I asked him to help me choose bulbs with the flower showing. They are expensive which is why I have not had them before and today I bought four.

They are arranged where they will be planted under the plum tree, waiting, because I am too tired to dig right now. Because the front garden has a colour theme the back has many colours and these pink-striped flowers among the Christmas lilies should be beautiful especially with the purple plums in greenery above. Perhaps I am waxing a bit lyrical. Yet, my mother used to say: 'Look at nature when you are thinking of making something. Nature never gets colours wrong. Look at the colours in a plum tree; the pink blossom, the maroon and dark green leaves and then the purple plums.'

As a result, I sewed a zigzag-striped tapestry evening bag with those colours.

Everything is so long ago. As you can see, many of my memories are three, or four, or more, decades ago. When my late mother-in-law, Gwen, used to say such things as she had first met a friend thirty years ago, I was, if not quite astounded, certainly impressed that anybody could have lived so long to have such a memory. Now, thirty years ago seems a mere bagatelle and I speak easily of fifty or sixty years in the past and, when I do, the ghost of Gwen hovers above in my memory. Because when she spoke those words it was, in fact, nearly fifty years ago.

And next year, my son will be fifty. Now, I think of him surprising me when he was ten months old, creating a strange noise, as I stood at the kitchen sink in a three-roomed flat behind our dry-cleaning shop. I looked up and behind me he arrived pushing his playpen filled with toys through the door from the other room, crushing it into a diamond shape as he pushed it like the infant Hercules towards me. His first steps.

Thursday, 9 September

Twelve eggs today. I am waiting for 100 per cent; thirteen eggs from thirteen hens. Closing in now on target. One hen is laying long thin oval eggs. Is it egg-bound? These are like no egg I ever saw and I am a poultry farmer's daughter.

Yesterday, Lindy and I visited the poultry pavilion at the Royal Show. Beautiful Barnevelder hens stood alone in cages, big-boned and striped in tan and black like something from the 1930s which Wallis Simpson might have worn. Also, the mighty roosters, white, red and black, almost as huge as turkeys and full of testosterone, crowing with their heads upright, combs crimson, trembling with hormones and stress.

I would love to have a rooster to fertilise the eggs here but the crowing means it is not possible in the suburbs. I consider buying some fertilised eggs from the hairdresser who has a rooster with her hens. Could I get a hen to go broody and hatch the eggs? I have always liked bricolage. To change one thing into another. Jam, preserves, olives, cheese and so on. To have eggs transformed into chickens would suit me down to the ground. Then, though, there is the problem of male chickens. What is to become of the roosters which hatch from the eggs? Would I kill them? Am I hard enough to kill and eat what I have bred and is of no further use? I am. I respect scruples in matters such as this, but I don't have them.

In a town near where I once stayed, the name of which I can't remember, there was a haven for abandoned roosters in the bush. The main road out of the town went through this place and there, among tall gum trees, were dozens of roosters which had been brought out of the town and let loose to live out their days in a masculine haunt like a monastery among the trees.

Wednesday, 15 September

On the matter of beans: today I planted a row of French beans which had sprouted among two layers of daily dampened paper towel on a plate. This was because only three seeds of the first lot (which were purple French beans) planted a month ago had sprouted.

I must be one of the few people who don't like eating broad beans. Yet on Saturday when I went to lunch at Gay Bilson's home she had cooked broad beans which came from her garden, mashed them with olive oil and put them into little bowls along with bowls of peas in their shells which she'd boiled and dressed with olive oil. There were globe artichokes also boiled and dressed and everything was delicious. I think it may have been so good because it was all freshly picked.

There were bowls everywhere; on the table, on wooden shelves among books. All handmade and it all looked surprisingly modern. I had felt that pottery had gone out of fashion but this was beautiful. The truth is, that when things are loved and collected with an eye for style, they have an aura. What's style? It's the way you wear your hat. And what are aesthetics? It's the way you fold a sheet.

Outside was a garden full of food plants. It was an unusual shape because there was nowhere to stand and admire the whole. The great, late, Australian landscape designer Gordon Ford wrote, 'Do not clutter the void.' Wise. But here, there never was a void to be cluttered, nor was there meant to be one. The whole garden was surrounded by a circle of native flowering shrubs: grevillea, Geraldton wax. Naturally, lots of birds, too.

Summer

CHRISTMAS (2)

The persimmon tree is heavy
with green balls
the Mariposa plum in her white net veil
is a bride stepping shyly towards her husband
the tall fig.

Today the sea and sky merged
and a white sail glided on
like a disabled angel
Lindy and I could see our toes
in the cool clear water.

All this, and yet I still need
the miracle of forgiveness.
Patience is the sweetest ally.

Hope and faith are rocks
piled beside the everlasting sea
which is as blue as my girl's eyes.

I see now I could joyously follow
with my bleating sheep
that star hope.

2011

Summer

Monday, 24 January

The day of the salvias. In Jerry's garden I saw a brilliant midnight blue salvia which I immediately longed to have in mine. Today I saw one in a pot at Bunnings nursery which is a short bike ride away, and although it cost a lot, I bought it. Called 'Black and Blue'. A horrible name, like a description of a beaten woman. There were punnets of a more common salvia called 'Mystic Blue Spires' thrown out for a dollar each so I bought a few of them, too. When I began this garden two dark blue salvias went in and they are now enormous. Salvias bring bees. These are all planted in the front garden now and it is exhilarating to have it done. Is this the sense of accomplishment a cave woman felt when she brought back a good haul of roots or seeds to grind after a day searching? It feels atavistic, a deep sense of achievement, more than is really justified.

How strange, the telephone has just rung and when I leant over to put it back in its cradle, I saw a hen, standing beside me, pecking at the wooden floorboard. She has got out of the pen so I must cut her wing feathers again. They are quiet companions, with a pleasant air about them, although I know that if I fell down dead in their pen they would eat me. I think I wouldn't mind. Useful to the end. That would please me.

Monday, 21 February

It has been a beautiful summer. Barely a heatwave, although yesterday and today have been over 40 degrees. (It was 50 degrees in the shade yesterday on my brother Bill's verandah at Stockport in the north.) The sunflowers are ready to pick. If left too late on the stem, as I've said, the seeds fall out and the ants carry them away. I watch carefully and cut one or two of the great pale green suns daily. Then I carry them like plates to the chooks, brush off the froth of hundreds of small flowers which cover the black concentric pattern of the seeds and lay them down like an offering on the hay. The chooks then go to work.

Self-sown 'Kent' pumpkins have risen from compost and grown up through trees and out onto the footpath, also over the gravel in the back and the cement down the side. Cucumber seedlings of three kinds, apple, long green and Lebanese, were thrown into the bin at the nursery over a few weeks and each time I asked and was given them. The satisfaction of resuscitation is enormous. There is nothing I won't do to save a free plant, or any plant for that matter. The trick is to know what to do; in some cases it is I who is killing the plant.

Lindy and I have long conversations on why her rhubarb wilts, why her lime tree has stopped fruiting (a vine has put it in shade) or what ails my dwarf cumquats, mistakenly put in the front hedge when I thought I was buying normal ones. Or why for the second year our French beans won't thrive.

My late friend Julia Britton, the playwright, and I used to walk between her house and the Henley jetty to the Semaphore jetty. On these walks she counselled me on what to do with my leftover life after divorce. She suggested that I enroll somewhere, matriculate, and then go to university. Astonishing news to me. I took her advice, went to a matriculation school, and then enrolled in Classical Studies at university. This was probably the most influential advice I've ever taken. It changed my life.

She had said to me, 'If you study the Classics, you will always have something to think about.' It's a curious thing to say and I don't believe I have found it so, but if you have a garden you can always be puzzled.

Once when Julia and I were visiting the Experimental Art Foundation, which Ian North, Donald Brook, Noel Sheridan and my late husband founded, we stood in front of a performance by an artist who had covered himself in honey and lain down in a glass box of bees. Julia turned to me and said quietly, in her droll way, 'Oh, that's not new. A Roman empress did that in the second century.'

Spring

Sunday, 16 October

You may have noticed there has been a lapse in my book of the hours, and I think I should explain why, although I would prefer not to. I have been depressed. It creeps up on you. I didn't know I had it. But one day riding home from the supermarket with salmon for lunch I suddenly wondered if I might be depressed. I'd had insomnia for almost a year but I did not actually feel unhappy, because I think depression is not necessarily unhappiness, not happiness either, but in me, a strange feeling of irritability. I said to Paula who was staying with me, 'Paula, do you think I could be depressed?' And she said 'Yes!' with such alacrity I said I would go to the doctor as soon as the clinic opened on Monday and I did. Whether it is the medication, or being able to sleep, or simply time, or a combination, I can't say, but today I swore I would start writing again. A good sign, surely.

When I was sixty, I thought, 'When I am seventy I will be entering old age.' Now that I am seventy I think, 'When I am eighty I will be old.' That is how ageing has affected me. As many old people also say, they do not feel it and so this is how I trick myself or my good health tricks me. Perhaps it is all only vanity and refusal to admit the truth.

Two weeks ago, I caught the community bus for the first time. I had booked a seat to go shopping as it occurred to me that riding with my bike panniers full of six bottles of wine, a big hard cabbage, a shoulder of pork and much else would one day affect my balance. I decided that this was foolish and since the bus often glides past my house, I would be wise to use it before having an accident.

A revealing scene ensued when the bus arrived at my house. A woman who looked about ninety came to the front door and reminded me, as I left, to lock it. Used to dealing with the absent-minded or confused, I supposed. When I went to get on the bus she took my elbow. I almost shook her off like a dog. A thrill of insult ran through me. When I sat down I realised that I am now sensitive to acts that show somebody thinks I am so old I am incapable. She had meant it kindly but I did not like it. We were dropped off at Westfield shopping centre at Marion.

When the bus returned three hours later, I had a trolley filled to the top and above, with a dozen bottles of wine, a garden hose, 25 litres of potting mix, food for a fortnight and library books. I'd had a pedicure and a manicure with no thought about how the shopping would all fit on my bike. I had left the library until last and ran across the parking lot with the trolley zigzagging out of control.

As the bus drew up, I went to its back door, ready to unload the shopping. However, the ninety-year-old and Barry, the bus driver, told me to get onto the bus and together they loaded on my shopping. When we drew up at my house I hopped out and said, 'I'll get the wheelbarrow.' But by the time I had brought it out Barry had loaded my things onto the top of the closed lids of the rubbish bins put out for collection. I filled the barrow, forgot to give him a gold coin for the cost of the trip and came inside.

So now, once a month, this is what I will do. And I'll hold my temper about kindness which was not meant to be insulting, though I have wondered if it was also a brag.

Thursday, 20 October

Under the quince tree, strawberries are ripe. I eat two or three daily, straight from the plants: they taste sweet and whiten teeth. (Eating bananas whitens teeth, too.) Coming indoors with a few strawberries, a couple of leeks, some limes and a few sweet peas reminds me that a garden does not have to be prolific to give food and flowers daily. It is better that the crop comes in small batches.

Turning to sweet peas, I have to admit that not a single plant on the wire at the back fence lived. The chooks ate the lot. They seem to love legumes. All those special varieties—the sprouting of them between damp paper towel which was so successful. All went for nought. However, the French climbing beans now growing there would not have thrived if the sweet peas had, as there'd be no room. Yet, beside the lime tree on the western side, sheltered by the iron fence, two sweet peas have grown and are in flower. I learnt a lesson. Again I vow that the chooks stay in their pen unless the gate springs open after I have closed it, as has happened sometimes.

Long oval eggplants have gone in and four apple cucumbers along with English spinach and 'Grosse Lisse' tomatoes from the seed box. There's one Diggers heritage purple and white striped

eggplant planted, too, and it cost as much as the six others altogether. And now it's warm and raining softly. Birds are calling and
it's dusk.

The buff-banded rail has gone. It disappeared about a month ago.
Topknot pigeons in the front garden may have harried it away, or it
could have been just time to go where it was meant to go. It may
come next year.

Shirley poppies, big bushes of them where the bird used to hide,
are in bloom and what a surprise they are. I never saw a more beautiful poppy. Some are double, some single, all are the most lovely
colours. Watermelon pink, scarlet, white edged with pink. Let me
go and check. Yes, some are pure white, others vieux rose and some
white with an inch band of tomato red. Bees are at them all day long
so I will save the pods for friends. These poppies are the easiest,
loveliest and most surprising flower I ever grew.

A new thing I have discovered. And that is, if you are in the
habit of having a drink before dinner and want to cease this for a
night or a while, if you have dinner at about five o'clock or as soon
as you come in the door, or as soon as you feel hungry, you are
not likely to feel like a drink. This can, of course, mean having
dinner pretty soon after lunch, but I find that it works. It's not the
alcohol your body wants, it's the carbohydrate in the alcohol. So
if you eat, the mood for a glass of wine vanishes. Just thought I'd
mention it.

Tuesday, 25 October

Watching a dog trainer on television, helping people control their
unruly dogs, I suddenly saw that in many of my relationships with

men I have been as silly as these people. I mean, the trainer points out that the dog needs to be made aware that it is not the leader of the pack. The owner needs to establish that. It struck me that this was my mistake. Fawning and oozing charm at their dogs, the owners let them lie on silk sofas, sleep on their beds and disturb them during the night. They feed them when they bark and indulge every whim of the dog while having their own life upset to such a degree they are at their wits' end. Some people in desperation take their dogs to another town or suburb and dump them. Others just go on living in this dog heaven and owner hell. This can, I think, happen with cats, too, as one of my friends gets up to feed her cat during the night when the cat lets her know it wants to be fed.

I have said elsewhere that I have never met a man who is not truly terrified of his own wife. Yet, in my own case, I have always been the one who is not in charge. This may be why I am so happy making a garden on my own as nobody is here to make me plant what I do not wish to plant. Not that my own husband was a tyrant, far from it. But he was, in fact, in charge. When we married, he, having been to sea, said: 'In our marriage, we are, in a manner of speaking, running a ship. There can only be one captain and I am that captain. You are the first engineer.'

Intrigued and delighted at the originality of this, I agreed with alacrity.

Now I have the freedom which comes to many in old age. Neither captain nor engineer, I am merely the mother, grand-mother, aunt and gardener, single with friends. Determined not to harvest regret.

Monday, 14 November

Bees in the trees and in the blue salvias. Sparrows are chirping in the plum and the chooks are laying eleven or twelve eggs daily. Rosie, the new black hen, waits her turn at the nest in the shed where she and the white ones roost at night. Of four nests, only one is chosen by all. Some failing restaurateur probably understands this. One red hen is only laying occasionally and when she does the egg is sometimes long like a 'Kipfler' potato.

As you see, I can't call them 'it' any longer. Affection has grown and to call a creature 'it' when you have intimacy with it daily, especially when it is ill—investigating its orifices, nursing it and watching it day after day until it keels over or revives—is hard to do.

'The last shall be first,' I say to Rosie, bullied away by a red hen from a pan of milk-soaked wholegrain bread. I toss a morsel of meat to her behind the red hen's vision. Rosie deeply lacks initiative. The more she succumbs to the harrying, the more she has to endure. It is too late now for her to change so I try to smuggle in those little treats. Awfully like people, wouldn't you say? If the red hen protested, I could add, 'Have I no right to do what I like with my own? Why be envious because I am generous?' (Matthew 20:16). Could the red hen learn? Could we?

Sometimes, when gathering eggs, these oval miracles of design and purity, I marvel that from these birds, which live only on bread and milk, mixed grain, cabbage, lettuce, shell grit and scraps of meat, comes daily this holy perfection which fills my hat at three o'clock.

Last week I used fifteen eggs to make The River Cafe lemon tart for the wake of Lindy's husband Robert and I thought how much he would have liked it. He was a sailor who served in the Korean War.

'Always lifting the lids of the biscuit tins after dinner, even though we've had seven vegetables with meat and dessert,' Lindy said.

He was a loved and lovable man. He could sew and could make an eighteenth or nineteenth century military uniform without a pattern but had trouble lighting the fire. Lindy's huge, beautiful garden was a mystery to him but he stood among it raising and lowering the flag daily as if on board his ship.

Tuesday, 15 November

The courage of the frail elderly who glide along with their Zimmer frames crossing the road among thick traffic to the shop, or pushing up the ramp towards the doors of the supermarket, makes me admire them. One white-haired man, almost doubled over, pushes a frame jerkily up a low ramp in a way that seems impossible because the geometry of his body and the ramp are so taut that it looks madly audacious as he perseveres against gravity and frailty.

There are carers now for such frail people and it is they who wheel the trolleys of groceries alongside their client and who stretch up to bring things from the shelves.

One old woman shopping alone had a bottle of mineral water, a bag of lollies and a carton of tea when she stood at the checkout to pay. She worried me. Perhaps she just came for the outing. Shopping malls and supermarkets have replaced cathedrals as places to pass the time.

When my late husband Richard and I had a little dry-cleaning agency and greeting-card shop at a bus stop, old people would stop and talk to him. One hot summer morning Richard asked a friendly old woman with only about two visible teeth, 'How are you planning to spend the day, Mrs Neece?'

She replied, 'I'm going to take a Bex, drink beer and watch the cricket until I pass out.'

We were both twenty-four and impressed.

Tuesday, 29 November

Zucchini are the next vegetable I want to have again this summer. Three plants went in this morning; they have either dark green or yellow fruit and, warming to the idea, I soaked ten or more seeds, then put them into the seed box. Some years, in common with other plants, zucchini thrive; and in other years, they are covered in mould and do no good at all. Just the same as the sickly eggplant and tomatoes in this garden last year.

Wednesday, 30 November

For days I have been replanting self-sown orange cosmos into the front garden and hacking out buffalo lawn intruding among the plants and trees. I see now that I am like a chook myself, scratching deep into the soil, ripping away with a fork and my nails. Perhaps, like dog owners are said to look like their dog, I will begin to look more and more like a hen.

I had a tender moment this afternoon and let all thirteen hens out for an hour or so while Lindy and I sat and talked. Having sworn they would not be let out again, I thought that it wouldn't matter because they had escaped recently and I had not yet raked up the chaos so they might as well have an hour of joy before I went to work. It must be good for them and perhaps they find minerals and grit which makes them healthy. They lie, fluffing their feathers in an ecstasy of a dust bath, anywhere they can make one, looking so like my brother in a hot bath after a day of getting cattle onto trucks. Lindy and I laughed as Rosie took a hop, step and jump right over a red hen lying fluffing herself under the apricot tree.

Today, I took the green wheelbarrow to Mitre 10 nearby and brought home 30 litres of ti-tree hay to spread when I clean out the chook yard. I have taken a sniff through a hole in the bag and it smells, as I had hoped, slightly of ti-tree. Alex at the shop pumped up the tyre of the barrow for me and repacked the pump to sell later. He said, 'You won't get this service at Bunnings or Woolworths!' To show gratitude, I ran back into the store and bought a beautiful hanging basket of hundreds of deep blue petunia blooms which I'd admired earlier. It is hanging outside the back window and it looks sensational.

Summer

Thursday, 1 December

In the morning, lying in bed writing my diary, a piece of wonderful music was on the radio and it made me think how lucky I am. How wonderful it is to be my age and have no pressing reason to rise. No need to hurry, nobody needing anything from me. Then the announcer said Graeme Koehne was the composer and that my friend Peter Goldsworthy had written the lyrics called 'Mass for the Middle Aged'.

When Lindy and I sat talking yesterday, discussing among other things the solar garden path lights I've been given, she told me, laughing, about a friend who is even more frugal than us. Her friend has invented a way of saving electricity by pulling up the solar lights in her garden at dusk, bringing them indoors and using them to light a room. We laughed about this but when I told my friend Dinah today she thought it was a brilliant idea for somebody who was poor. All you would need to do, I suppose, would be to put the lights into an empty jug to hold them upright. Needless to say, I want to discover if it works, so tonight I am going to try it. Because there are only two lights in the garden, they will probably shed too feeble a light for this to be of any use. I am quite drawn to crankery.

There is nothing to show of progress for this day so far, except this report, because I have spent the time chasing wild birds away from the hens' food and, in between, coming indoors and trying to discover how to make double spacing on this document, with no success in either.

At the window, a dove is making one of my favourite sounds, a thrum of cooing. It always seems to be a warm quiet afternoon when the doves or pigeons begin cooing. A small, peaceful song.

Why do some of us feel we must, in spite of what I wrote earlier about lying in bed, have made some progress daily? To have something to show that you have lived this day. That is what diary writing is about. To have planted something, to have fed something or somebody, or given somebody something. It could be a country thing. My mother and the mothers of my friends fed, delved and gave daily almost to the end.

It might have been a bowl of soup to a workman or to a child, or a bunch of flowers to a neighbour, or some eggs, or almonds: just anything that could be a gift. In the case of my mother, it was a sponge cake she made five or six mornings a week. Beating eggs in the Mixmaster on the table behind her while she was washing up. As soon as the cake cooled, it was sandwiched together with apricot jam she made from her tree and with cream she had whipped from her cow. Now there's a thing which cost almost nothing and which didn't need to be changed, as different men came to eat it.

The men were from various places who called in as part of their work or others who worked intermittently on the farm. For instance, the grocer who came to take the order for the week's groceries. Or Max, the chicken sexer, or men from the Department of Agriculture, or just somebody calling in, wanting to buy eggs. All were fed. Even the doctor. In her great old age, my mother had him up on a stool in the kitchen bringing down jars of jam to take home to his family. As a result he forgot to take her blood pressure.

We four children know plenty of her recipes and I have her hand-written recipe book, but the maddening thing is none of us know how to make our mother's chicken giblet soup. We try, but we can't make it like hers. One trick was grated carrot put in for the last two or three minutes, I remember that. And egg noodles and a dry soup mix with yellow peas in it. Lots of chicken giblets and sometimes, if she had them, chicken feet. Parsley, I remember that. Onions. But ours is not the same and we do not know why. It is not that we are, as you may suppose, so romantic and nostalgic that nothing other than this soup made by our mother will do, no, it is not that. We just cannot get the same flavour.

Friday, 2 December

'Oh! How sweet the smell.' This morning I cleaned both the chook shed and their yard and, opening the ti-tree hay container, the lovely scent wafted out around their yard. The white hens and Rosie roost and spend most of the morning in the shed to let them feed away from the red hens. They had a bale of hay and an hour later they had spread it, saving me the work.

I watched a red hen yesterday at eleven in the morning (which is about the time poultry settle down to rest) nodding off as she sat in the doorway between the shed and their yard. The greyish eyelid appears to rise from the lower lid upwards as sleep slips on. For all the world like a person nodding off on a train with those little alert jerks when a bird called or another hen brushed past. Her head went so slowly down that only by watching how her comb lowered against the line of a brick in the wall was it possible to see the depth of sleep arriving.

Again and again another hen would brush past and, though I wondered that it did not seem to irritate the sleeper, it did not make her move. It is a meditation, to watch chooks as they eat, scratch, doze or boss each other.

Rosie, this most elegant black hen, knows that accepting her role is not necessarily upsetting, it's just a matter of waiting behind the others eating the food and revealing only her back view or a side view to one of the angry red hens. Rosie may outlive the neurotic red ones. With acceptance as calm as a Buddhist, having abandoned retaliation and greed, Rosie is a lesson in patience and humility. This hen deeply lacks ambition.

Saturday, 3 December

Today I heard the first carol on the radio. Later, Lindy and I ate my first, and only, two apricots. They were delicious and even though both apricots had been broached by birds, it made me see what was missing in the dozens that might have been on the tree if I had not fertilised it with barrow loads of hay from the chook yard. As we ate, Lindy asked if I had fertilised the tree and said that she had heard on the radio this morning that this is what causes the tree to be barren. Just like the blood orange, as I said, which since it has had no water, mulch or fertiliser has dozens of green fruit.

Monday, 5 December

A white hen was dragging her tail on the ground this afternoon and crouched as if it hurt to stand upright. I brought her in and made a sick room of the shower alcove which is enormous. The hen sat there on newspaper with a bowl of water and some grain mix. Her eye was bright and her comb a good colour, her respiration not much faster than my own as I held her against me, bringing her indoors. Her left foot turns inwards and this caused the hen to stand upright like a Peking duck and when she walks, she favours the left leg as she limps.

Peter said, as we sat on his back deck at dusk when I asked his advice on what could be the trouble, 'They live or they die.' I wondered if it might be a calcium deficiency as these chooks eat more multigrain bread soaked in dripping and milk than they do bought poultry food or mixed grain. He said that if I used only the layer feed which he brings me, the chooks' diet would be complete with all the nutrients they need. But this doesn't always appeal to the hens. They get bored with pellets. The tremendous amount of lettuce and cabbage leaves I get from the supermarket bin must provide quite a lot of calcium. I rode off, not sure at all what to do to help the sick hen, except to leave her alone overnight to rest and let nature take its course.

Tuesday, 6 December

Opening the bathroom door and peering into the shower alcove, I saw that the hen is alive and looks a bit better. She has eaten some grain, spilt the water and has diarrhoea. I cut up cheese and put in a carton of baby's yoghurt to see if that might help. She ate some of both and then she squatted down and slept. Like all sick creatures, she sleeps most of the time.

Having the shower occupied I hosed myself down beneath the bigger plum tree then went back to do matron's round. The hen looked drab, her feathers dirty from fluffing up dust and hay as a way of cleansing. I gave her a bath in the wash basin full of warm water with washing powder dissolved in it. The hen sank down as if the water was comforting. I rubbed the feathers with a block of Sard Wonder Soap and the water turned dark grey. Then she had a warm rinse and was carried out in a towelling bath mat to dry in the sun.

The hen staggered off into the shade and began energetically pecking at gravel which may mean she is desperate for calcium or small stones to grind grain in her gizzard. I burst out laughing as she reminded me of an ancient grandmother bravely lashing on her apron, knowing children were coming and duty must be done.

My friend Peri is eighty, makes three meals daily for herself and her husband who is still going off to work at eight, five mornings a week. When I asked how long they could keep going, she said, 'I suppose we will keep on until one day we just fall down.'

I thought that the other chooks may lack calcium, so I let them out. *Carpe diem!* Seize the day! they seemed to cry as they rushed past in a river of feathers. Pebbles of gravel flew in many directions as they ecstatically dug. They made dust baths and lay in them like people luxuriating in a sauna. How can I, no matter how many times I declare they must stay in their pen, not let them out occasionally? The best practice is not to let them stay out too long as that is when they wander down the side into the vegetables and begin rioting.

It is dusk now and the white hen looks angelic, so snowy compared to the others. It is as if she has been prepared for heaven. I would not be surprised if she is dead in the morning because, back in the shed, nature can take over and, as with all creatures, only the fit survive. Although I did once see a bull at Tucker's place standing under gum trees with its leg bent in a sideways 'V'. I asked what had happened and was told that the leg had been broken and it had healed into this shape. The bull was otherwise perfectly well and ready for market.

Thursday, 8 December

Hard to believe that yesterday I didn't write you a report on the sick hen but something happened. First, though, the news is the hen is alive and eating.

The reason for the delay is that, riding to the supermarket, I saw a sign beside a big pile of black soil lying in a driveway between large open gates. It read: 'Help yourself. One tonne free vegetable soil.'

Rushing home, I rang Lindy who said, 'I'll be there in a tick.'

I hastily took the wheelbarrow and six plastic buckets along with shopping bags and hurried back to the soil. Already an old man was shovelling the soil with his hands into a small plastic bucket and another was spreading some on a lawn opposite. Lindy drew up in her small white car with Cathy, her daughter, who has a farm at

Kadina and teaches dressage. They had horse feed bags and a dust pan as in her haste Lindy could not find the spade.

A four-wheel drive drew up and a young woman got out and another came with a barrow. We lowered that tonne in half an hour. When the owner came out he said he'd like to be able to close the gates (which the pile of soil was blocking) by nightfall. There was not going to be any doubt about that.

Lindy and Cathy took home my filled buckets and bags and their own and returned for more. I took the barrow home, thinking how lucky it had been that the man at Mitre 10 had pumped the tyre. We were jubilant. Beautiful sifted fine black soil for free. Lindy is going to replant her vegetable garden. I began straight-away, spreading the bags of soil under the plum tree to cover the roots of the roughly transplanted hellebores which were above the hard gravelly ground. That pile of soil was the best Christmas present Lindy and I could have.

The limping hen maintains herself away from the others, resting in a corner of the shed in a hole of hay that she has dug. Now it looks as if she will survive and maybe, with rest, the twisted leg will mend.

Friday, 9 December

A warm, wet day like a poultice. I am among the few who can remember mustard plasters which parents laid across the chests of children with colds, asthma and croup. Nobody mentioned flu in those days. Did it do any good, I wonder? It would have calmed the parents and the child, being a tender thing to do: that must have helped.

Last night, across the railway line, Christmas carols were being sung. I opened the front door and the windows and lay in bed listening. They were young voices, perhaps a school. As you can see, it is summer and so far, I am happy to say, peace reigns.

Today, two men from the council came and have lifted the grapevine at the back door up onto extra wires which extended onto the roof. The newly grown hanging branches are now tied up and make the green sail even bigger. It is beautiful. This service from the council is a marvellous thing. I have dreaded having the house grow shabby around me, waiting for a ceiling to sag and gutter to rust. This help, which only costs $10 an hour for the work of two men, has made me believe I can stay in this house as long as my health holds. The men will also prune my trees if I need it. In fact, they said that most of the work they are asked to do is pruning.

Saturday, 10 December

The sunflowers that I sowed from seeds in the poultry grain mix are now taller than me and have big green heads forming which the chooks will enjoy when the seeds turn black.

The chooks have begun, or one has, to eat their eggs. Yesterday two eggs were sticky with yolk on them. Today four were in the 'Bless this Nest' kennel and when I gathered them later there were only three. I think this means more shell grit is needed. Though there is dolomite in a carton in their yard and they do eat that, it may not supply enough calcium for them.

This discovery means eggs gathered several times daily. Once this vice starts, I hear, it's hard to stop except by whisking the eggs away quickly. It's a nuisance because it means that more time will be taken up with playing around in the chook yard. I stand and watch them with such pleasure and visit them about ten times daily. Now more than ever I need to go into the shed and take the eggs. Deborah, Duchess of Devonshire, kept hens until recently and only gave up after a lifetime because they became too much work for her. She and her sisters, the Mitford girls, kept hens when they were children and sold the eggs for pocket money.

I have been wondering how long I can keep this up. When I said to Peter, who has about fifty hens, that I find it a lot of work, he said, 'I don't find it much at all.' Well, he has an automatic watering system which only gives a couple of centimetres of water in its circularity, and which gathers dust from the hay over which it hangs, as well as an automatic dispensing bin of pellets. He throws them some wheat at dusk. This, apart from the wheat, is the professional way.

I'm with my mother on this. She was a stickler for clean water. Every hen which blinked, our father used to say, had its head chopped off before it could blink again. This was because when our parents bought a poultry farm and hatchery, the fowls developed an eye disease which could infect the others and kill them. Their life savings lay in this so every hen was precious. We ate the ones which had the misfortune to blink in front of our mother.

CHRISTMAS (3)

Overnight it rained.
The blue hydrangeas take it
as birds drink from their parents.
It's always like this, sudden changes
even in drought—as the angel gave Mary

the shock of that lily. And I tell people
the story when they stop at the gate
asking the name of the lily.
It's news to them and they pass on
puzzled or glad I can't tell
(I hear there's a new interest in these tales
that mainly only the elderly know).

The post girl chugs past on her bike
wearing a Santa Claus hat—giving always goes on
so she's frantic.
Love has never been lost
it just got confused. The physics of faith
pealed out in those carols the choir sang
last week at dusk as Joan and I rose to our feet
to sing with the people
'Hark the Herald Angels Sing'.
And here the rain is still pouring down
filling the buckets
I eagerly placed on the lawn.

2012

Summer

Monday, 2 January

Sleeping with a fan. The family have gone home and it is over 40 degrees. The chooks pant under the apricot tree which, from their fertiliser, provides deep shade.

The brugmansia's long pale leaves, wilting, look like green kid gloves against the galvanised iron fence which gets the afternoon sun. Lindy and I walk an hour or two to the beach, swim like elderly duchesses then shower, saving our own water. The day heats up. I have been given a water tank for my birthday. Hugh and Cathy ordered it and next week it will arrive.

I love the summer and now can see that those old plants, lion's paw, aloes, olives, plumbago, Russian and Mexican sage, can stand almost any amount of heat without being watered. In the city, why did we ever start on all the thirsty plants when this is a dry climate? It seems, like the settlers, we could only see the landscape as a European would and made our gardens to match. Of course, at first we had plenty of water, most houses had tanks and many had wells or bores. People were frugal with their water. Being a country child, I was ten before I saw a garden sprinkler. They've been banned here for years so now most small children do not know what they are.

The farmers' wives in the outback, observing what was really going on, may have planted soft things but they learnt, being close to weather and truth, that only drought-proof plants would survive the summer heat. I cannot tell you the pleasure it gives me that Ron, the council volunteer who, with Nathaniel, came to mend things in the house, said that the garden reminded him of one at an old farmhouse. Yet at the back of the house and down one side there are plenty of trees and plants which need water. Nobody's perfect.

Monday, 9 January

I've got a sick red hen. Thrice, I cut her wings for she flew over the fence and then scratched out plants from pots at the back door. Having cut even her tail feathers so she could not possibly have any lift, I saw that she was bleeding from her prolapsed vent. Then I understood. The others had been pecking it and even with her shortened wings she had to escape.

'With terror's light wings did I o'er-perch these walls. For stony limits cannot hold terror out,' she might have said, paraphrasing *Romeo and Juliet*.

Ashamed to have cut her feathers so severely, I took her in and gave her a warm eucalyptus bath in the wash basin. Then I gently pushed the prolapse back and felt inside the vent from which the egg emerges into the cloaca to see if she was egg-bound. There was an egg but further up, not blocking anything.

She rested in the shower alcove a few hours like the white hen with the turned foot which is now walking well.

The sick red hen passed a little blood so I gave her another warm bath, cleaned the orifice and now, to compound the illness, she has diarrhoea. I got out Great-aunt Dorothy Venn's oval-topped bottle of calamine lotion and poured it over the prolapse which had re-emerged. I swear that the hen knew I meant well. The calamine lotion seemed to help and I left the bird in the shower alcove on a towel, with newspapers, water and grain.

There have been no double-yolk eggs, so it just may be that laying an ordinary egg proved too much for her. Or, it may be that the heat caused the diarrhoea which caused the prolapse. With the exception of conversation, nursing a sick hen is exactly like nursing a person. Sometimes I find myself, before entering the bathroom, knocking on the door. I go in and out, wondering what I will find. When I put her in the sun to dry after the bath, she seemed to be falling forward in a sort of faint. I examine her, see if she has eaten, urge her to drink and depart.

I have slumped into old age like a drunk entering a wine cellar. It didn't happen overnight but until recently I was able to ignore many signs. But now, arriving in full array, age has dressed me in its drab beauty. Today, as I was about to step onto an escalator, a woman, whom I thought was close to my age, glanced at my face then stood back and waved me on.

I was on my way to Joanie to hear a Mendelssohn concert. Sitting there, looking over the lines of the grey-haired audience, I remembered that when Adelaide Writers' Week began and I was in my twenties, I used to be amazed to see so many elderly people together. I'd nursed a lot of elderly people but had never seen the sight of those grey heads en masse. Grandfather Llewellyn refused to go to the Adelaide Repertory Theatre Company and when his wife Gwen asked him why, he said that all the audience were too old. She pointed out that so were they. But he didn't go.

His son, my late husband, refused to go to any picnics or parties held for the victims of poliomyelitis. Ninety per cent paralysed himself, Richard did not want to be seen with anybody with a disability. I did understand that and felt much the same. We were desperately trying to be normal. It was the struggle of our lives.

At that time, in the 1960s, there were few young people in wheelchairs but as diving and car accidents grew in number and medical care got better, more and more people used them. Yet, about twenty years later and with a new degree in sociology, Richard was appointed Disability Advisor to the state's premier. As a result, he worked for the next decade or so with hundreds of disabled people.

It seems that this denial of my own ageing is common but now the day has come when I must face it. I look old, I feel young and I love riding my bike and I am heading for eighty. Now Peri is having her eightieth birthday party next month in Sydney.

Thursday, 12 January

I'm a wreck. The hen and I lay low today. She in the shower alcove eating noodles and I watching cricket on television. Nursing is hard work. I had forgotten. At dusk I put the hen out to eat sunflower seeds and to enjoy fresh air and sunshine. She lay on her side as if collapsed, warming her orifice. Because sunshine has healing properties, I had exposed her vent to the sun yesterday to try to heal the wound. The sun, as you may know, sterilises and heals wounds. The hen seemed to enjoy it as I held her there. Now here she was, doing the same. Clever bird.

Friday, 13 January

This morning, while fiddling around pulling small green fruit from the cumquat trees (to encourage them to put on leaf), I smelt smoke. I wondered if it was something burning on the stove. But, no, I realised that it was Rome burning and if I didn't go indoors and get back to this book, it will never end.

After a swim this morning, Lindy and I called in on Peter to ask his advice about the hen. He said that she would never recover and that if I put her back with the others, they would eat her and she must be killed. Call me squeamish but I asked my brother to kill her. I have chopped off the heads of many chooks, but in this case it did not seem right, having knocked on the door of her refuge and nursed her, that it should be my eyes she saw as the blow fell.

She spent her last hours this afternoon under the plum tree scratching about and I did not care what she dug up. She had a few happy hours alone in the garden. Then Peter came with a small axe and the hen, seeing him, fled. I checked that his axe was sharp. In *The Decameron* a woman buried the head of her lover and planted basil over it. That might be a fitting tribute to this hen which I am sad to lose. It seems strange that, out of thirteen, one hen could drown in a bucket of water, as one has, another twist her foot and another develop a prolapse. A farmer would not pay for many pairs of school shoes with figures such as these.

How did my parents do it?

Saturday, 14 January

It is raining. The new tank will have water pouring in. I have been out tapping the side and cannot tell what I am supposed to hear. There just seems to be, even at the lowest rungs, echoes. All my childhood I watched people knock on tanks and seem to know what the sound meant.

Saturday, 21 January

Another hen has presented with a prolapse. This time it is Jemima, the white one with the turned foot. She seems sicker than the other hen. For two days I did all I could to save her but she grew more and more lethargic. The same potions were poured on, but she ate nothing, drank nothing and in the end I could see that she was dying. She had one peaceful afternoon and night in the garden under the apricot tree with a shelter of towels built up to shield her from the sharp wind. In the night she moved in among the beans as the wind changed direction and there she sat breathing gently with her eyes closed. She gave up the ghost. When I came home from my birthday lunch, the hen had fallen on her side and was dead. I buried her near the other hen, beside the apricot-coloured brugmansia to fertilise it. So they did not live in vain.

Both laid eggs enjoyed by friends, neighbours and me. What is it that money can't buy?

Answer, fresh eggs.

Friday, 3 February

It is always intriguing to realise that you have been staring at a change in the garden, or for that matter, in your life, for days or months before the situation becomes radiantly clear. For example, now that the grapevine has completely shaded the back rooms and thus all the pots of petunias and herbs near the back door, nothing thrives anymore. I had been wondering why things looked so lank and wispy. Now I see it is from lack of sun. Therefore, today I bought gardenias and begonias. For the first time I will have shade. This is the only garden I ever made that, for four years, has had no shade except lately under the stone fruit trees. With such ardour and sudden strength I rooted out all those weak plants which I had replaced thrice trying to get them to flourish and in went the glossy green gardenias and the little red and white begonias. It now looks clean and healthy, as if the owner knows what she is doing.

Sunday, 5 February

It rained in the night. I heard the water gurgling loudly in the drainpipe and gloated. The eastern coast of the country has had colossal floods and we, in contrast, have had a few light showers. Peri rang from her farm in south-east Queensland and said that the Tallebudgera River at the fence of her land has broken its banks and the house is surrounded by water as it was when we were there together in the 1980s. Then, the mud on the lawn came up to our ankles as we walked out in our pink nighties to see. After days of tropical rain and hearing the weather forecast for more, Peri had said, 'Don't worry, I've had the house restumped and there's a new tin roof.' This time she said, 'All the citrus near the river have been standing, drowning, for days.'

Tuesday, 7 February

Clogs at the front door, clogs at the back. Even we now have a little mud and it is glorious.

I remember digging up arum lilies for my garden from a creek at Woonona with my friend David and singing the Flanders and Swann song, 'The Hippopotamus', about mud. I sang to lighten the situation as, blundering through mud up to our calves with a spade each, losing a shoe as we went, must have been uncomfortable for him, not being able to see. Yet he dug where I showed him a clump of lilies and we walked home, pushing a dripping barrow load of lilies each. He followed my voice when we went astray, as for part of the way there was no path, only a paddock. I went back and turned him straight again. Game for anything, he showed me that there's nothing a blind person can't do.

Now I am off to have a few bowls of my friend, cook and food writer Belinda Jeffery's soup, called 'Very Addictive Chilli Bean and Chickpea Soup', which is on the stove.

Monday, 13 February

'How can you say to your brother, "Brother, let me take the speck out of your eye" when you yourself fail to see the plank in your own eye?' (Luke 6:42)

Yes, I thought of giving up watering Barbara's lemon tree slowly dying in its pot at her door, where I'd returned it, over the past few weeks. It seemed that I was only giving it the death of a thousand cuts as, whenever I saved it when it wilted, it soon collapsed again. I could not understand how, having to pass the tree to enter the house and with a hose attached to a working tap nearby, the neighbour could leave the tree to die. Maybe, I told myself, she has depression. That makes two of us.

Yet, since Barbara did not know what an apricot was when I showed her my tree two years ago with fruit on it, nor what sweet peas were when she saw a fence covered in the flowers, I could hardly blame her for not knowing her tree was dry. But the truth is, I felt impatient. A lesson was soon available.

Wondering, for the umpteenth time, why the cumquat trees have failed to thrive no matter what I have done in the way of stripping off their fruit, watering, pruning dead twigs and feeding them, like a child with undiagnosed coeliac disease, they have failed to thrive. One evening, while pulling out some buffalo grass from around a particularly sick tree in an attempt to get more water around its roots, I noticed that the grass roots, hidden in the soil, were actually almost choking the tree. Once I began to dig, great lengths of buffalo emerged. Piles of drying roots now stand around every tree. After a fortnight of digging at dusk until I could barely straighten, the trees are liberated. Now maybe they will thrive.

If you wonder why I dig at dusk, it is because wine gives me strength. After a couple of glasses of red I feel emboldened, even reckless, and walk out in the cooler air, not intending much, but find that I can work much harder than at any other time. It must be the carbohydrate.

Wednesday, 15 February

A blow: another sick hen. Seeing the bloodied feathers at the rump of a red hen and calling out to nobody, 'Oh, not again!' But this time, it wasn't a prolapse. (I know now that is a death sentence.) Rather, this was an almost bare rump with a few feathers wet and red. She'd been pecking herself. So, back to the bathroom. The warm wash in the basin was comforting and, as the others did, she sank into the water showing the feelings of relief General Gordon would have had had he been relieved in time. I poured more calamine lotion on the bare red skin with the few pins of feathers remaining and left her to stagger around the back garden in the heat.

Each washed hen develops a fit of pitiful shivering, even though they are in the sun. They lie as if stunned. I let this one lie there trembling and then turned her over and up she got and walked away. This third hen is not kept in the shower, which I think of as the intensive care unit, but stayed alone overnight sheltering behind a grapevine's trunk. This is more like a convalescent ward and if she recovers and walks around the garden scratching in the earth, it can be the rehabilitation unit.

Naturally, all this amuses Peter and Bill, my two younger brothers. They think it's hilarious. Tucker is in the north and I would not bother him with these tiny events when he deals in hundreds of thousands of creatures. When the RSPCA recently prosecuted him for not shooting almost a thousand cattle in the drought, which had water but not enough feed, he said to me, 'What about the 87,000 I saved?'

At his kitchen table on Boxing Day, he said to me, 'You know, drought is like war. You have to manage it with triage. There is no use trying to save the dying. You must save the living. You can buy feed, but not in the substantial amounts that are needed for large numbers of animals.'

In other words, the owners of smaller holdings can buy enough to save fewer animals. But when there are tens of thousands, it is pointless buying small amounts of feed only to give them all the death of a thousand cuts. The animals must be shot.

However, at the end of the case the RSPCA brought against them, they, Patricia and Tucker, were found not guilty.

I have ridden to the chemist and bought a tube of antiseptic ointment containing lignocaine which is, as you may know, a local anaesthetic. I ran the cold tap on the vent and bare skin of the hen, thinking cold water might calm the itch. After it was dried, I rubbed the ointment into the red skin of the hen and if she pecks at that, she will have a numb tongue. So goodnight, sweet dreams. Please drink some water. I have spent half the day following this hen around with a bowl or a bucket of water and only tonight did she take thirteen sips. 'Push fluids' was written on almost every patient's chart hung on the foot of their bed when I nursed. I say it over to myself as I lug the bucket around.

Thursday, 16 February

A glorious day full of bounty.

I gathered a bag of ripe figs from the tree on a vacant block in Glenelg. This was the same tree from which the cuttings were taken only two or three years ago, one of which now screens my kitchen window. I left some on Peter's doorstep and am making figs in syrup from an old Barossa Valley recipe. It's easy to do. It is boiling on the stove, all hobs of which have only one temperature lately and that is red hot. It is a matter of moving it away, like an alchemist, to lower the heat and save it from boiling over. This must go on for three hours.

The recipe says to use six dozen figs to three cups of water and to boil that for twenty minutes. Then grated fresh ginger is added, about three tablespoons, and two and three-quarter kilos of sugar. It is boiled for two and a half hours and then a cup of vinegar and the zest and juice of two lemons is added at the last thirty minutes. Frankly, I did not count the figs because, after all, what is it but fruit in syrup and I was in a hurry. I poured in four kilos of sugar and let it boil. My mother used to put a spoon into a jam jar before the boiling mixture was poured in. This saves heating the jars to sterilise them in the oven and stops the jar from breaking from the heat. Strangely, for this recipe the jars must not be made airtight so cellophane paper dipped into vinegar is tied over the tops.

Friday, 17 February

I lost the red hen. Searching over and over, round the garden under every bush, she was not to be found. Was it a fox? The man at the supermarket whose mother lost all her chooks to a fox had warned me of them but there were no feathers around; though, admittedly, this hen had few enough. As you see, this flock is diminishing. As the Spartans said during their war with the Athenians, 'Our numbers are thinning.' Giving up eventually, I fed those in the pen and went to look for eggs in their cupboard. There was the lost hen sheltering from the others although, at the time, it seemed that she had gone home to lay.

Later I found no eggs but more bloodied feathers. She can't drink or eat in the shed or pen because if she does, she must turn her back to the others. Rather like a politician. I took her out, gave her another bath, dried her with the hair dryer and all the while she watched herself with some interest in the mirror. I applied the new cream and laid her on her side in the sun to give the skin exposure and warmth. Again, she shivered but not, I think, from cold, but either from shock or a nerve in the leg on which I laid her because, when I stood her up, she trembled no more. All this means that until her feathers grow, this hen must be put into the chook yard every evening and the others into their shed with the intervening door closed so that she can't be pecked. How long will I keep this up? Beguiled I may be now, but for how much longer?

While all this was going on, feeling that the day was drifting away and nothing was being achieved, I picked the last of the plums from the blood plum tree to make chutney and boiled them in the leftover syrup from the figs preserved yesterday, with more sugar, lemon juice, two cups of balsamic vinegar and some cardamom seeds, two chopped onions, pepper and salt. It's turned out to be sensational.

'Nothing's wasted' (meaning experience from one's life), as Victoria Glendinning once said to me, explaining how she became a biographer after having been earlier employed interviewing women in London slums.

Speaking of waste, I'm saving barrow loads of cuttings and planting them in the dry earth outside the railway line's fence across the road. It's good soil and I use only plants that are in my garden. I'd like big trees.

Saturday, 18 February

The signs aren't good. This hen is sleepy, listless and off her food. She is pecking her feathers. She does, though, drink morning and evening. I think she's a goner. Like the white one which fell over dead, this one seems content to huddle down out of the wind beneath the mandarin tree, waiting, I think, for death. I can't face asking Peter to give her the *coup de grâce* because she seems peaceful and is no longer pecking at herself. Let nature take its course. But what am I doing wrong? It may be that they have too much greenery, which I was warned against. Watching their happy rush when I toss in a bag of 'Iceberg' lettuce leaves that I get from the greengrocer makes it hard to ration them to a few leaves daily.

But I always overdo things. Even when it was my turn to feed the fish in their bowl in the schoolroom they all died because I gave them too much food. That was a nasty feeling, knowing I was to blame. I imagine goldfish were not easy to come by in a country town at that time.

Monday, 20 February

Lazarus! Thinking to find the hen dead this morning, or close to it, she had a surprise for me, scratching in the dirt in an energetic way. Looking perky. But how long can she go without eating? Two days ago, remembering the Indian doctor in New Delhi who cured me of dysentery overnight with antibiotics and plain yoghurt with salt, I offered yoghurt but she declined it. Then I boiled spaghetti, which all the chooks love, with some salt and sugar, hoping to replace her electrolytes, but had no luck with that, either. The others fought over the pasta when it was poured into their dish.

Walking out of the front door with a bowl of water for the hen, I found Barbara's dying lemon tree in its pot left on the step. I think it is a gift. She has left it like an orphan on the step of a church as she is unable to care for it. A bit unnerved, because it is as if Barbara read what has been written about this tree, I took it around to the shade of the grapevines, pruned it, raised the level of the soil with extra potting mix and gave it a bucket of water containing Seasol. It's weak, like the chook. Live or die, I say. Too much fussing around over weak things. But my heart is in it.

Lying in the sea yesterday, I realised that this is a very good time in my life. I thought that I have not yet lost any close friends to death, although a few have drifted off, and I have let one or two others go. I am not yet at the stage Aunty Beck was at 103, when almost everybody she had known through her life, except her children, had died. She was busy making new friends at Resthaven village and even they disobliged her by dying. She kept at it til the end.

Aunt simply stood up to fetch a cushion for her chair, slipped, then fell and drifted off after a few final days of serenity, giving her now large family of descendants time to come. She had written her order of service funeral plan in the church where she had worshipped, chosen the hymns and directed that her coffin was not to be present. Which I thought an original and mighty piece of tact to spare the grieving. Her stepson Rob and I drove away and he, a man as orderly as she, paid the funeral director on the way home. Then we called in at the chemist and Rob paid her final bill.

Wednesday, 22 February

Yesterday a friend suggested I try the internet for advice on what ails this hen. I wasted a lot of time with no results. However, things are looking up, even though, after days, the hen will not eat. But the antiseptic cream from the chemist has helped and the bare rump skin is no longer bright red so she has stopped pecking herself.

I went off to mow the lawn. Clouds of dust rose thickly until I could not see at all. I plugged on and now the garden looks orderly, like a bedroom after the bed has been made.

Friday, 24 February

Miss Lazarus has woken from her sleep and is eating heartily. I tried to put her back into the pen with the others but they had forgotten her and flew at her savagely, so now she can live in the garden and do no harm, I hope.

Saturday, 25 February

A house next to Peter's is being demolished and piles of beautiful old pink bricks lie in front of the bulldozer. Yesterday, I asked one of the workmen if I could have some bricks and he gave me six grey ones from the path. Yet it was the pink ones I wanted, but didn't like to say so as they lay in front of the bulldozer which was moving. So today I have been back and lugged bags of pink bricks into Peter's garden so that he might bring them here in his car. I can get three bricks in each pannier on the bike and brought home about eighteen. They are laid out to make a curving edge in the back garden and suddenly it looks structured and quite lovely. I am electrified with lust for these bricks. Lindy, on seeing them, said that they look Roman and they do, too.

Sunday, 26 February

After we swam this morning, Lindy used her car to load up pink bricks and we filled it until it sank and she thought it dangerous to load up any more. As soon as we got them home, I laid them out, continuing the curve. When that was done, I made a long straight edge down the side where the oranges and limes grow. Then I went back again and again, filling the panniers until I could do no more. I feel, you see, that the bulldozer will finish levelling the site tomorrow and, being Monday, the truck which takes all away will finish the job. So it is today or never.

Finally, in desperation, I borrowed my brother's big green rubbish bin and wheeled home forty kilos of bricks. A wheel came off so I dragged the bin, with the axle screeching against the asphalt road. Then I returned my own empty bin to Peter, hoping he would not notice it wasn't the same shade as his own. The bricks were laid out immediately as I am exhilarated by them. These bedding edges are going to be beautiful.

I see now that stages of stiffness and muscle pain are not necessarily always a permanent part of ageing. A year or two ago, when making a garden at the railway station in Woonona, I was often stiff with an aching back. But all of this has simply faded away. A friend who is a GP said to me one day at a party, 'Why are you limping?' I said it was because there was muscle pain deep in my buttock.

She told me to get on my bike in a different way, not forwards, but backwards. How to do that, I don't remember. Yet the pain faded and I forgot that it was ever there until it returned, briefly, a year or so later. I am telling you this, in case you feel, if you have these signs of old age, that they are to be your companions forever. Perhaps they will be, but not necessarily.

instinctively. Secreted away, silent and serene, the broody hen floats like a ship on the nest. Her comb grows paler daily.

Sunday, 11 March

It has been a beautiful summer in Adelaide. The eastern states and the north have had floods but we have had mostly sweet mild weather. Day after day it is 27 degrees. The air smells of autumn in the early morning and always has a whiff of sadness to it.

Dawn is silver and black with a huge, low, silver moon surrounded by a pale gold circle.

I have bricked the broody hen into her nest like a medieval saint attached in the same manner as to a church. Saint Viridiana, here she is, secret, silent and serene going about her business. I did it to protect her from disturbance by the others.

I have learnt that a hen has an egg vent like the back of a neat, small white envelope. A perfect design. They did not copy our stationery, but they might have. If you stuck a stamp on a hen's breast and pasted an address there, you could post her.

Having the hen locked in with two bowls of water with a stone in each so that it is harder to spill, and some food, means I need to check her daily when gathering eggs from the others. If I die, she dies. Just like a bricked-in saint's dependence on her keeper. How long did those women last in those terrible rooms? Some went mad, that is true. Perhaps some achieved rapture. Some, ecstasy, maybe. What did the bishop think? Who paid for them? Some were, no doubt, from wealthy families. Perhaps it was one way of escaping abuse, as in the case of this white hen. After all, it is a nunnery out there and vicious to boot. The truth is, I have smuggled in sperm hidden in those eleven eggs.

Wednesday, 14 March

Back with my old friend Louise to Perry's Fruit and Nut Nursery. We strolled around while Louise chose an avocado tree she had ordered. We tasted the figs and dried goji berries left out to try. We had a picnic of a brie and pear tart from a recipe by Belinda Jeffery in an olive grove with a thermos of tea.

There is a legend that if you fall asleep under an olive tree, you dream of healing. My friend Diana said on the phone when I asked her about this: 'Asklepios, the God of healing, whose daughter was Hygeia, set up sanctuaries. It was considered auspicious in the ancient world to sleep there as the god may send a healing vision. There were dormitories around sacred pools so that in sleep he could appear to the sick and heal them.'

We did not stay but drove off to three other nurseries that Louise knew. At one, I bought a curry-leaf tree which, I learnt, differs from a curry bush. The former is used in curries. Later Louise slid a cardboard box with its base open over a tall gardenia to protect it in the car. I planted it in a big pot at the back door.

This year, as you know, gardenias at the back of the house are going to be my new thing. Already, some are blooming so I sleep with the smell of one or two flowers in a cup. Even though it has been four years, I am still learning what will thrive here and what will not. Until there was shade from the grapevine at the back, gardenias would not have done, but now, they are just the thing. When the vine dies back it will be winter. The sun then will not harm them.

Good news. A big self-sown 'Queensland Blue' pumpkin, weighing over five kilos, is sitting on a plate on the dining room table. Barbara Santich, the food writer, said in a talk last week at Adelaide Writers'

Week, that 'Queensland Blue' pumpkins are peculiar to Australia as they are a hybrid bred early in our settlement. I think of this pumpkin as security against winter.

In this street, speaking of food security, seven houses have been knocked down and two new houses built in the place of each one. I love thinking of the clean bathrooms and kitchens they have in place of the old. In the new gardens installed by the landscapers, again not one food plant is present. The elderly owners have left and young ones with children are here. A plum tree, an apricot, any citrus would give the children free fresh food and memories of those trees all their lives. Please plant a fruit tree; they cost no more than those awful modern ornamentals. And they take no more water.

Monday, 19 March

Because there have been broken egg shells on the nest, the broody hen is let out at eleven every morning now as I thought she may be eating the eggs. Maybe madness has arrived early. There are only six eggs of the eleven remaining. When the cupboard door is opened, she won't emerge at first, lying there drugged and full of lassitude, doped on her hormones, her comb pale as an old plate, she just wants to be left alone. But later, she strides out, terrified now of me, scratches in the hay, eats a little, sips water and then I push her back into the cupboard, watching through the crack in the door as she settles on the warm eggs. Because of her hibernation, this hen has become a stranger to the others, who fly at her. So now they must be let out into the garden to let her have her exercise in peace.

Wednesday, 21 March

Happiness is mine. An hour ago, as I lay listening to a Phillip Adams program on Multiculturalism from Perth Writers' Festival, Peter arrived. In his hands he held four red hens by their feet like a dark bouquet. I raced out and we walked together towards the chook pen and shed. All the old hens were in the yard, except the broody white one on the nest. He handed the two bundles of legs to me. Their yellow feet were like daffodils and I let them go down onto the hay as gently as I could. They are point-of-lay pullets, six months old. They felt soft and young in my hands. I said, 'This is your new home!' Frankly, I felt proud. Hay, nesting cupboards, a perching rail and clean newspaper on top of the cupboards, it felt like welcoming somebody to your house.

I had not known, you see, that these four would come today. I had asked Peter a month or so ago to buy me some new chooks when he went to his supplier but they were sold out. I mentioned multiculturalism because of the coincidence as the other hens went berserk in their yard. They were cackling and calling as never before. Yet, they, too, had once been new here and the white ones, especially, had been put alone in the shed to protect them from the red hens for weeks. And so it goes.

More now than ever I see that we humans are sometimes no better than the birds of the air when it comes to accepting strangers in our country. Poultry has no religion or philosophy, as far as I can tell, yet we can act the same. Now the tally is fourteen hens. However, this morning as I let the broody one out for exercise, there were not six but only five eggs left. This is either the clumsiest hen ever, or she is hungry and eats the eggs in spite of food and water being locked in beside her. I must have faith and wait.

If no chickens emerge, I am toying with the idea of buying a dozen day-old chickens and putting them under the hen. That, or buying another dozen eggs from the hairdresser and trying again with another hen. I remember my mother putting a hen that was not necessarily broody into a nest and putting fertile eggs under it. The hen seemed to then become broody. I think the hen was blocked off from the flock while this was going on and so she had no alternative but to let the hormones swirl in and to slump down into the sleep that brings life.

Friday, 23 March

And then there were three. From eleven eggs, three remain. At this rate, there will not be one left to hatch on the 29th. However, I now let the hen out twice a day and this, I think, will stop her consuming the eggs. How surprised she will be when, and if, a chick emerges. The last and only time she ever saw a chick was when she was one among hundreds in the hatchery. I always thought that a cow must be surprised when a calf emerges. Yet the cow immediately knows what to do and shows no surprise at all; it just licks the calf in a tender, welcoming way.

I have been planting white onions. They were sitting up above the soil in the punnets, tiny white balls, smaller than a child's fingernail. Today I filled the four seed boxes with beetroot, spinach, orange pansies and a packet of Mr Fothergill's seeds of frilled Shirley poppies which were such a success last year. Also, pansy 'Victoria Rococo' with 'huge, crinkly double crushed velvet blooms' and blue poppies, both from Erica Vale seeds. It is easy to write these names, but another thing to bring them to fulfilment. 'Talk is cheap,' as my mother said.

I found these Erica Vale seeds when Joanie and I went to Oliver's Pets and Plants. I was asking if they sold day-old chickens, in case there are none from the last three eggs. Yes, they will have some, if the hatching is successful, this Friday the 30th. But they are awfully dear. Ten dollars each. You can buy a two-kilo dressed chicken ready to roast for that price. Knowing that not all chickens emerge from their shell at the same hour, or even the same day, the 30th would be suitable because if they are needed, I could ride over and bring the new ones home in a box. How I will keep it flat, I don't know.

Wednesday, 28 March

One day to go. The hen is still on the nest. I press one of the warm eggs to my ear every time I let the hen out and strain to hear a sign of life. Nothing, so far. But they seem to be bursting with promise. Packed with a perfect, small, damp form with a beating heart and a beak ready to peck a way out. Luckily, it is a nurse's reunion lunch tomorrow.

Thursday, 29 March

Hatching day. Nothing. A big, fat nothing. Perhaps tomorrow. Lindy's daughter Cathy advises that sometimes it can take another week for eggs to hatch. That means a month. I never heard of that. A male emu takes fifty-six days to hatch eggs and they are enormous, five or six times the size of a hen's egg.

There is, though, new life here, because tonight, watering the seed boxes, I saw dozens of Shirley poppies have spotted the black soil with green.

Friday, 30 March

Today my sister-in-law Patricia, giving me advice on the hatching of chickens, told me that when ducks are sitting on eggs during a heatwave, if the temperature gets over 40 degrees, the duck, having left the nest briefly to stretch, eat and drink, returns and does not sit on the eggs, but stands above them until the heat lessens.

At lunch at Eros cafe yesterday, I told my friend Emily that the hen had eaten all but three of the eggs in the nest she was sitting on. Emily said, 'Perhaps the hen felt that she would not be able to cope with so many chicks.'

I laughed and laughed as she meant it seriously.

'I don't think the hen has any idea of what may come out of those eggs,' I said.

But now I wonder: if a duck can be so wise, what might a hen know?

Sunday, 1 April

Daily the bigger lime tree flings down one or two perfect fruit and it seems a marvel to have this gift when lemons have been failures and both limes now thrive. Do not, unless you are a genius at growing seeds, bother with the rare blue poppy. Having now read the instructions on the packet, it seems unlikely that any of the ten minute seeds will sprout. They need cold and darkness. Here, apart from inside the refrigerator, there is heat and light. I have hidden the egg carton full of seed-sowing mixture in which they were sown in the laundry and do not hold many hopes. But success or failure is in the mind so I will remember to keep them moist or negative thoughts will affect the outcome as they do in so many other matters. Now, suddenly, I remember writing about trying to grow blue poppies years ago. I get these fads.

Having just run out to check on those 'Rococo' pansies, there are none up yet, but they should be comparatively easy to sprout. Ants were about, so the egg carton is now elevated to protect the seeds. At least there are no possums or rats here as there are at the house where I had dinner last night. It was not a topic for dinner, so now, the report on those three eggs remaining in the nest.

It is about three days over the time they were due to hatch so I removed them, and opened each one. The first was a white egg which was probably laid in the nest the first day by another hen so it was, let's say, past its prime. The good news is the other two were fertile as they had formed chickens in them which probably died about the tenth to the fourteenth day. This means that I can try again and, with all that has been learnt, will perhaps have success.

Putting those half-formed chickens in the compost bin seems pitiful, as all new creatures, having had no chance at life, always seem. No use thinking of the rich life they could have had here, scratching under the plum tree or digging up the newly planted vegetables down the side. Provided, that is, that they were not roosters.

The hen seemed unaffected by the loss of the eggs. Pale as a ghost from her long internment, the comb only a faint pink, she is now a nervous wreck and squawks like a teenager, wings flapping when another hen or I come near. Motherhood takes it out of you.

Wednesday, 11 April

Two blue poppy seeds are up. It feels almost miraculous. Finding them this morning I rang my friend Jane, yelling the news down the phone. Now she wants to buy the seeds, too.

Tuesday, 17 April

I heard on the radio how jacarandas and wisteria came to Australia. It was the Colonial Secretary, Alexander Macleay, who brought them with him in 1826. He got the jacaranda seed from South America and the wisteria cuttings from China. Having grown both in his garden in Surrey, England, he brought them here. He also brought the first coriander, cumin, dill and port wine magnolia. But Chinese people were likely to have already brought some of these herbs when they came here.

Heaven bless the person who brought blood oranges. The tree down the side of this house which would not flower is now bowed down with five, six or seven tennis-ball-sized fruit at the end of every branch. I can't make myself thin out the fruit because it is so precious; so if a branch breaks, it breaks. No colour yet on the skin, which means it could be two or three months before the fruit is ready. Then I'm going to buy a bottle of Campari.

Tuesday, 24 April

The first cold day and welcome, too, a feeling of zest and a sting in the air with rain in the night. The tank is half full. I knock, knock with my knuckles on the corrugated iron rings of the tank to hear where the water level makes a dull sound. Above, it echoes emptily. A flock of starlings flies up from the newly mown lawn. A willie wagtail hops around in its cheerful way and a Murray magpie flutters down and then up. When pruning the apricot tree a while ago, I found a small bird's nest high up in the tree. I left the branch in case the bird uses the nest again. A sparrow flew into a dense olive tree in the front garden and, thinking it may be nesting there, I have been out to search but, apart from a small crop of green olives, the tree is empty. A flash of green and a lorikeet flew out.

So many limes have fallen that, seeing Indian lime pickle today at the supermarket, I decided to try to find a recipe. Jane has made her big crop of persimmons into chutney using the *Green and Gold Cookery Book*'s tomato chutney method and says that it is delicious. I will do that with my crop which still, so far, no bird has touched, thanks to the double layer of netting. For weeks the netted fruit trees have swayed in the wind like demented, disconsolate brides.

Tuesday, 1 May

This afternoon, wonderful heavy rain. The front lawn is flooded and the ground at the back door, too. A man arriving to mend the oven was drenched and his tool box as well. I dried him off with a bath towel as he came in the front door. The wonder of rain. What would happen to us if rain failed to come, not for a decade or two, but forever? How long could we last? And what would be the point? Perhaps we would rely on the desalination of seawater. What this thought means is that I was overcome with gratitude at the silver water pouring from the sky.

Luckily, I had picked all but four or five of the persimmons which I left for the birds. Now there are thirteen jars of persimmon chutney on the kitchen bench made from Jane's tomato chutney recipe. I'd give it to you here but I think that any tomato chutney recipe would serve to use for persimmons. Maggie Beer's green tomato chutney recipe would be perfect.

Thursday, 3 May

A pair of New Holland honeyeaters have been flitting through the red and brown leaves of the grapevine outside the back bedroom while I lay watching. There must be insects in the dying leaves which they are hunting. It was an error to prune some of the vine about a month ago, because it led to browned leaves which can't be untangled from the living ones and so there is not the scarlet stained-glass ceiling effect which was there last year. I won't do that again. Trying to keep leaves from covering the back area is like trying to hold back the sea. Day after day sweeping them up is now a pleasure and it made little difference to have filled a bin with the cuttings earlier; it merely spoiled the raving loveliness of autumn colour.

The smell of lime, onion and mustard seed chutney is filling this room. Every now and then I stir it with a long wooden spoon and wonder where I will get the jars in which to keep it. Maybe Peter has some. He's tired of making jam now and when I offered him a bucket of quinces he declined. He did, though, give me a recipe for his delicious chocolate bread and butter pudding.

Tuesday, 15 May

Glorious days. Bright, cold mornings. Dawns of silver and black.

I'm elated after a visit to the doctor. The reason I went is that on Sunday nine friends came to lunch and next day, Joanie, who was formerly matron of St Andrew's Private Hospital in Adelaide, rang and asked me to go to the doctor. She'd noticed at the lunch that I have developed a habit of a small cough or grunt which she explained can be a symptom of heart failure.

I had noticed this new, weird little habit of mine, too, and thought it was a sign of ageing; something that the elderly do as their minds hum a little in an unselfconscious way. It was perhaps a sign of neurological changes or of asthma. But nothing of the sort.

When I tried to illustrate it to the young Chinese doctor, it was surprisingly difficult to do it accurately. He ran a stethoscope over my chest through every nook and cranny, took my blood pressure and pronounced that the heart was normal, there was no arrhythmia (which had been there before) and he found a chest which he seemed to think was like a huge empty granary. Not that he said that, but he gave me to understand that there was nothing there.

I rode home exultant and have been light-hearted ever since. Truly, I feel like turning cartwheels.

To top off this good news, it's now announced on Radio National that if you have had cancer, it can save you from Alzheimer's disease.

And if you have Alzheimer's disease, it can protect you from cancer. I suppose that the former is the thing to hope for.

Last week I planted tulips, having said yet again that I would not buy any more. Also, blue hyacinths and two dozen daffodils for the pots at the back door. These small annual rituals mark off the years and make me feel blessed that they keep going on, as one day they will not.

As I've said, my mother washed and ironed the twenty-eight shirts my three brothers and our father used every week and the ten sheets the family used plus everything else. But by the time she died, she no longer washed anything except her saucepan, in which she cooked fresh vegetables. She'd take them in to the communal dining room table for her lunch in the retirement village where she lived; they served reheated roast meat cooked the previous night and she also found the vegetables unsatisfactory. She got her vegetables from Jim, her son's immensely kind accountant, whose parents also lived in the village. An example of 'where there's a will there's a way'. But the reheated roast meat defeated her because she had no oven. She said, 'Imagine! Reheated roast!'

Speaking of 'where there's a will'. When she was in the retirement village and she felt ill enough, my mother used to decide to be admitted to the Royal Adelaide Hospital. She simply telephoned an ambulance, said goodbye to a couple of other residents and waited at the entrance for the ambulance to come. She climbed in and directed the attendants to take her to the Royal Adelaide. Once, she was missing for more than twenty-four hours and the staff couldn't explain it to us at all. Finally, another resident told them that Mrs Brinkworth had left last night for the Royal Adelaide Hospital in an ambulance.

Winter

Thursday, 7 June

A few last vine leaves hang like red stars in the net of branches against the clear blue sky. I sweep the leaves that have fallen and the brown skeleton of the four mingled vines planted only four years ago becomes daily sharper and clearer. It is always the same; you think nothing much is changing in your life or garden and one day you look and see enormous changes.

The blood orange is hanging low with the weight of its bright fruit. Peri told me when I said the fruit was still sour that it will need further cold weather to sweeten it. I had thought sun made sweetness so that was a surprise. Now, if I can find somebody with a digital camera who will take a photograph of me beside the tree, I may be able to enter *Earth Garden* magazine's contest to win a year's subscription for a photograph of a gardener with their fruit tree. It was 5 degrees this morning and now most days are only 14 degrees so sweetness should come soon.

All those dozens of Shirley poppy seedlings I thought were in the seed boxes proved to be cabbages so now three friends and I have a crop coming on among our bulbs. I cannot understand how this happened.

The fourteen hens are well in their deep litter of hay and now lay eight or nine eggs daily, which I think shows that they are well, as laying usually wanes in winter. Rosie the black hen is a gleaner. She waits until even the new pullets have finished eating then begins. She pecks the food on the ground which the others have thrown around. So undemanding and humble, it touches me to watch her wait. I still toss her special bits of meat but she is slow to catch them and often others reach them first. I wonder if she is slow-witted. Even so, slow or not, she has won my heart above all others.

Friday, 8 June

Two of those almost mythical blue poppies were planted today in the front garden in the little egg carton cups in which they sprouted. There may have been more because all ten sprouted, but eight disappeared and, picking up the box, I saw two small slugs. I hold little hope but in the curious way nature works it may be that, like a snow leopard, one bloom, against all odds, will appear. These poppies turn hills blue in Bhutan.

In common with many others I have a thing about getting something rare to grow. Jane my old friend tried with a peony which she knew needed a colder climate, by daily putting ice cubes on the soil around it on the advice of her gardener. No luck. We shrug and say, 'Worth a try!'

Tuesday, 12 June

For three days I've been perfecting making pasties. Not all day, you understand, but over those days. On the first day I made the flaky pastry from my 1941 *Manual of Domestic Art (Cookery)*. The second day, I made the filling and baked three pasties for Lindy's and my lunch in the sun at the back table. Today, baking three more, I didn't use the fan in the oven because it had dried out the pastry and these were better. I rode with them, hot in one of my panniers, and Peter, Helen and I sat down and ate them. You could say, with relish.

This pastry recipe is simple enough for a child as long as they have the strength to roll it out. And it's easy enough to remember because it's just plain flour with a pinch of baking powder mixed into it with water. Then butter is added. It is one half the amount of butter to flour. Just enough water (the recipe says one gill for one pound of flour but who now knows what one gill is?) to mix the flour into a dough that can be kneaded into an oblong three times as long as it is wide. One-third of the butter is chopped and strewn over the dough with a half-inch margin all round. Then it is sprinkled with extra flour and folded into three. The pastry is then turned round with the closed side to the left hand and rolled out into another oblong three times as long as it is wide. Another third of the butter is spread over, more flour sprinkled on, then it's folded and turned around again. It is rolled into another oblong, the last third of the butter is spread on the flour, and the final fold is done. This makes four folds of three layers each. The pastry is then rolled out into the shape needed.

Because this is from a school book and so needed to be baked during the lesson, or perhaps because it was from a time before chilling pastry was common, as there were no fridges, it was just put straight into a hot oven on a cold tray. But I left it in the fridge overnight and baked it after brushing the pasties with beaten egg yolk.

There is a footnote to the recipe which says, 'Never decorate the edge of flaky pastry as a cleanly cut edge rises much better. In a single layer of pastry there should be twelve flakes when baked.'

Today about fifty turnip seedlings were planted in the side garden around the citrus and among them lots of those cabbage seedlings which had mysteriously filled the seed boxes. If you feel sluggish, get into the garden. It is not only the second glass of shiraz that makes me feel spirited, it is the feeling of making new life. Out there at eleven, bent over, hacking through the couch grass in my sheepskin slippers and pyjamas, made a new woman of me. Or is it the vitamin B tablets or the antidepressants or a combination of all three? It could be the fabulous purple cattleya orchid which stands on the kitchen bench. It came from the orchid show on Saturday in the city where I went with a friend, Judith. The scent in these old halls where shows are held is like no other. Elderly gentlemen in cardigans and zip-up jackets who grow these orchids stand around ready to answer questions. Their wives make tea and coffee for the visitors, which comes with the price of the entry ticket ($2).

I hardly ever have $100 in cash in my wallet but I did on this occasion, so came home on the train with this beauty. It will get me through winter and much else. You may know, in *Remembrance of Things Past*, Proust used the name of these orchids as a euphemism for sexual congress. Speaking of that novel, I read in Rosemary Dobson's new *Collected* poems just out, that her husband read to her, night after night, that entire work and called it one of the great experiences of his life and she wrote, 'Mine too, mine too.'

Wednesday, 13 June

The silvery plectranthus in the front garden is overgrown so I pulled out several bushes and dragged them across the road to extend the garden I'm making there. The four brugmansia cuttings stuck in by the fence along the train line have new leaves and the prickly grey aloes show pink flower spires coming. I'm full of hope for this little spot as it should soon fill and then extend my garden in a way that looks natural. Another woman walking two King Charles spaniels went past and commented, 'Oh, I have been wondering who it was making a garden there.'

Thursday, 14 June

Wild and grey outdoors, like an angry woman. Remembering some ancient lore about dill curing upset stomachs I snatched some dill leaves from a seed box an hour ago. The dill helped almost immediately. How useful not having to go to the chemist, especially in this storm.

Now it's clear why those two hens died of prolapse. In *Gardening Australia* there is an excerpt from a new book called *Contented Chooks*. It says that too much bread gives poultry prolapse. And those birds had bread daily for months. I had been told that birds, even ducks on ponds, should not be fed bread. But I thought 'Fiddle de dee' and gave my chooks milk-soaked stale loaf after loaf and they gobbled it down. A white hen, one with an extended abdomen, proved, when I performed a postmortem on it, to have two fingers' width of white fat blocking its intestine. Almost a litre of clear fluid ran out from the incision. It seemed, then, that they had all been fed too much fat in the form of ham skin and dripping from roast meat trays. It's now back to lettuce which they love and the dull commercial food in the big yellow bags they do not enjoy. They eat that under sufferance when there is nothing else offered.

Sunday, 8 July

Taking the barrow to Mitre 10 to buy a bale of straw for the chook pen, I saw apple trees on sale and had to have one. The label said the 'Granny Smith' apple can withstand heat even up to that in lower Queensland so that is what I bought. Being so keen on growing food, I would have planted an apple earlier but did not think they would thrive in our climate. I rushed the straw home and returned with the barrow for the apple tree. It now stands inside the back gate, waiting until I get up enough energy to plant it.

Saturday, 14 July

Today at Bunnings I found a cross-pollinator tree for the 'Granny Smith' which has been planted outside the back gate. I did not know my apple tree needed a pollinator and possibly would not have bought it if I had, but later read the label which listed the names of the trees which are pollinators for it. The salesman reduced the price by almost $10 when I told him I'd paid less for the other tree at another shop. Determined to secure this bargain, I wanted to take the tree at once. However, I had not planned to buy it so there were 4 litres of olive oil in the bike panniers along with 3 litres of milk, 2 of vermouth, some meat and bread-making flour. The cashier said it would not be possible to get the tree, which is more than 2 metres high, onto the bike and that I would have to return to collect it because they won't hold things.

I knew that once I got home I would not feel like riding back so insisted that I try. She called for a young man to help and, while he held the bike, I bought a green bag with handles and he then put the tree into the bag and swung it from a handlebar. Planning to walk the bike I home, I wobbled off but after a while it proved so difficult I wondered if it might be possible to ride. I got on and glided home in triumph. It was not possible to plant the tree then and there, me being a spent force and hardly able to drag the fluids in, but at least I have the tree and one day, with luck, there will be apples galore.

Wednesday, 25 July

The second apple tree, a 'Red Delicious', is now planted out the front between the two olive trees which are its nurse trees. I learnt that use of the word 'nurse' from the late Roger Deakin's book *Wildwood* as he writes about trees which are planted to shelter other less hardy ones.

At dusk now I have a couple of drinks of red vermouth and soda with the juice of two blood oranges in each. Truly, I feel triumphant and grateful. Amazed, too, at such success. You see, the blood oranges are now ripe and so are the mandarins and the 'Valencia' oranges. All that fuss over these trees is now just a memory.

Monday, 30 July

We met by arrangement, Peri and I, both at the end of our rope, at Coolangatta Airport, she from Sydney and I from Hove. Peri's husband has been ill but he is back at work, at eighty-three years old.

Here, on Peri's orchard, the geese come up to the house, orange beaks lifted honking. Geoff the caretaker is away making a film on his life in Byron Bay, just south of here, so the geese are not yet fed. Four young peacocks hatched here peck at the new rooster brought in to fertilise the hens so he must be kept in a cage until he gets spurs and can defend himself. It is always tooth and claw.

A fox took four chooks a month ago because somebody forgot to lock them in. Geoff said, 'There are no foxes round here.' You cannot make a man do what he does not want to do. But a fox can. Only in Eden was there peace and that got boring for Eve. A woman needs a bit of frisson.

At dusk I light the wood fire, Peri makes a cocktail and I drink wine while we watch the sunset drowning in the bend of the river. (Beat that for a romantic sentence.)

EVE

Let's face it
Eden was a bore
nothing to do
but walk naked in the sun
make love
and talk

but no one had any problems
to speak of
nothing to read
a swim or lunch might seem special
even afternoon tea wasn't invented
nor wine

a nap might be a highlight
no radio
perhaps they sang a bit
but as yet no one had made up
many songs

and after the honeymoon
wouldn't they be bored
walking and talking
with never a worry in the world
they didn't need to invent an atom
or prove the existence of God
no it had to end
Eve showed she was the bright one
bored witless by Adam
no work
and eternal bliss
she saw her chance

they say the snake tempted
her to it
don't believe it

she bit because she hungered
to know
the clever thing
she wasn't kicked out
she walked out

Saturday, 4 August

Peri's ducks are laying so many eggs that she is giving them away and using them for cakes as they are reputed to be better for this than hen's eggs. For the first time I ate one poached for breakfast. It had a milder, creamier taste than a hen's egg. Now the challenge is to try the goose egg, as there are five on the bench because there are too many geese, so they were gathered to prevent the geese sitting on them.

Prejudices are strange. I dreamt I ate a dog in an Asian dish and woke horrified. My father would not eat rabbit, calling it 'underground mutton'. Well, what is wrong with that? Yet I quaver at a goose egg. Is it because it is so big I can imagine the gosling curled up inside? I'd like to eat one of these geese and yet to Peri it would be worse than eating dog as they are sacred to her.

Once when here on the farm alone, I was walking in to Elanora to shop when I saw a still-warm wild duck killed by a car on the side of the road. Waste not want not. I hid it in some bushes and, on the way home, collected it in a plastic bag. Having dressed it, I put it into a marinade of port wine, bay leaves, garlic and onions for two days. Then when Peri arrived I baked it in the marinade and it was delicious. Enough for two. I told Peri the story and she seemed to be happy to eat road kill. But, I think, not everybody would.

Wednesday, 8 August

Day after day I lie on the couch in the sun, looking out at the bauhinia tree reading copies of *Earth Garden* from the 1970s. Sometimes I laugh out loud. For instance, in Issue 9, June 1974, there is an article, 'How to Kill a Pig'.

1. Kill and stick the pig. 2. Bleed the pig. 3. Scald and gut. 4. Hang the carcass overnight. 5. Break carcass down. Then it goes on:

> I cannot stress too strongly how important organisation is. Check that all tools and equipment are lined up. A pig weighing 100 lbs feels twice as heavy, so try to carry out the job close to the pig pen. The less you drag the pig about the easier it is on you and the less risk of bruising the carcass. Having shot the pig drag him out as quick as you can and cut his throat. Don't forget to shut the gate after you in the inevitable excitement. (Or the other pigs will escape.)

It goes on to say that brawn can be made from the pig's head. Now, as one who has tried that successfully, let me say that you need a heart of steel to be able to look the pig in the eye as you put the lid on.

Telling my old friend Ianesco about this he told me that Winston Churchill had something to say about pigs. He said that he did not like dogs as they grovel too much, nor did he like cats as they are too aloof, but that he liked pigs because a pig will look you straight in the eye. You can say that again!

In this issue is a piece called 'Notes on Oats' with what must be the most horrid recipe I ever saw. It is Scottish, and called Kail Brose. 'Allow two tablespoons of oatmeal per person and one dessertspoon of vegetable oil. Toast the oats in the oil and pour on boiling cabbage broth (the juice in which cabbage has been cooked) stirring rapidly until it thickens in the form of knots.' Robert Burns probably ate this poor thing. Every time I walk past his statue on North Terrace I will send him a look of pity.

In the same issue is a piece on how to make a wooden loom to weave rugs, how to make wine from fruit other than grapes, how to use septic tank gas, and how to keep ducks. Issue 17 tells how to make an Aeolian harp, and soap, and build stone walls.

I now have a hankering for ducks as some breeds lay more than hens and they will hatch ducklings with ease. Could I keep ducks? Would my chooks accept a pair, I wonder? Ducks need fresh water to wash their feet and bills. And their owners must be willing to clean up the colossal mess if the ducks are kept in the garden because, unlike chooks, they seem not to eat plants so they can be left to roam. But they defecate about every fifteen minutes from what I can see of Peri's ducks. And, as for geese, people are not happy to have them in the suburbs because it is easy to see how they could save Rome, as their din is immense. Peri's geese sleep on an island in the dam far away from the house. They are never eaten or sold, just given away when the flocks get too large. (More than about thirty.) Peri calls them 'the soul of the farm'.

I am keen, you see, on breeding something. I will ask Peter to buy me a duck and a drake from the Gawler market when I get home.

Tuesday, 14 August

When Jane rang me at home to enquire about my holiday, she said when I told her of yet another friend who had fallen over, 'I get a surprise whenever I hear of somebody I know revealing that they are old. While I realise that I am old, it is always a shock to hear of others being old whom I knew when they were young.'

I had a chastening surprise when the taxi driver bringing me home from the airport rang his supervisor, saying, 'I have an old woman here who has lost her wallet.' This, at a time when I was dressed up and feeling slightly glamorous.

Spring

Wednesday, 5 September

The back door is rattling in the wind and the chooks are calling in their medieval-sounding language. Like a chant coming from an ancient yurt by nuns in feather cloaks. Magpies have been singing for days. So what could they be? A male choir in dinner suits. Small birds are flitting through the crumpled new leaves of the grapevines, catching insects, I think.

This year the two fruiting 'Thompson Seedless' vines must be sprayed with copper sulphate to stop the mould which ruined the crop last summer.

Bees came four days ago just as I was becoming worried that it was too cold for them to enjoy the white plum blossom. Then, on the first sunny day, dozens of them flitted through the tree and, when I watched later, they did what they are meant to do, and that is they went to the pollinator plum nearby and took nectar from that, too.

All these spring events happened as if clicked on by a machine. Naive, perhaps, to think this is all remarkable, but nonetheless watching it happen seems wonderful in a way I never found it before. As children find things in nature surprising, so, too, these things can come as a shock to the elderly.

Thursday, 13 September

Last night, I pulled up what I thought might be a thistle and found it to be a tremendous creamy parsnip a foot long. Inspired by this, today I filled a bucket with soil and a mixture of soaked 'Chantenay Red Cored' carrot seed and Yates parsnip seed. I'd read that because the carrot seed especially is so fine, it needs to be mixed with sand to save it from being sown too thickly and, having no sand, I used dirt. In *Gardening Australia* it said that parsnip seed has a short life and must be kept wet the whole time after sowing. It must be watered twice a day.

To save these, along with some French beans from last year's poor crop due to the chooks' clawed feet, which are like a long garden fork and can dig almost as deep, I dragged some metres of wire netting over the whole lot, watered it well and came inside satisfied. I'd found small oval 'Chantenay' carrots under the wire from a sowing months ago which I had forgotten and this, too, gave me the will to grow more of them. Now, reading the back of the parsnip packet, it says that a plank of wood should be laid over the seeds to keep them moist until they sprout. However, I strewed this lot around; there is nothing in rows. I wondered if a few dinner plates there might do. But I draw the line at that.

Another reason I am keener than ever to grow food is I am reading

The Second World War by Antony Beevor. To read of the millions
of Germans, Russians, Greeks, Poles, Japanese, Chinese and others
who starved is horrific. Beevor says that starvation is the quickest
way morality is destroyed. The Japanese were horrified when they
saw their Chinese prisoners kneeling eating grass and roots. Nobody
could read this book and keep one of the new gardens planted in
front of the home units and two-storey houses around here where
there is, as I have said, not a single food plant or tree. Everything is
ornamental. Try eating that or feeding it to your children.

Speaking of food, these twelve chooks have a new type of pellet
Peter buys for me that is entirely vegetarian. It has marigold leaves
in it to make the yolks golden. Now they lay ten or eleven eggs
daily.

Another hen looked poorly for a few days and then one morning
she seemed to be unable to stand. I picked her up to bring her inside
to the intensive care ward of the shower alcove but she gave a great
shudder and died.

A few weeks before I had found an old Stanley knife in the street
and picked it up, thinking it might be useful. Because, again, I
wanted to know the cause of death, I laid the hen down under the
plum tree. Remembering the large amount of fluid that came from
the other dead hen with the blocked intestine, I put this one where
her fluids could do the most good and performed an autopsy. There
were two enormous cooked eggs inside. Both too big to ever have
been laid, even though neither had a shell. They were cooked, I
suppose, because they were so long inside with her body's heat.

I remember seeing the chef Heston Blumenthal demonstrating
on television how to cook an egg perfectly by keeping the temperature extremely low and taking a long time. Little does he know, hens

had already invented it. What was upsetting was knowing that the creature must have suffered and it was my fault.

So there will be no more mucking about with their diet.

PARSNIP

Earth's long ivory tooth
in a buried smile
which becomes
winter's snarl
tugging at the hem of my skirt
as I walk by
looking for a cabbage
bending to see
into the heart
of the green thornless rose
that is not yet ready—
spilling earth
as it comes out.

A life spent in the grave
beneath a green fern
it lies on the path
like a fish
dying in the air

Walking indoors
shaking off the soil
that gave me this parsnip

to boil
all it needs now
is pepper and a bit of butter
but the hole most surprised
born in that wrenching moment
lies there gaping in the sun
dark and thoughtful

Saturday, 22 September

There is nothing more beautiful to edge a shady garden than clivias. Almost thirty years ago when I saw Peri's line of clivias reaching from her back gate to the front gate, under trees she planted which even then were 20 metres high, I didn't understand why it looked so lush and elegant. At that time in the Sydney Botanical Gardens there was a great curve of them. They were photographed for their calendar which hung in my kitchen at Balmoral Beach.

It is strange that these things which become so familiar are not necessarily understood until you attempt the thing, more or less by chance, and you suddenly see how marvellous the effect is. It is what has happened in the back garden inside the edging of those old pink bricks. This is because I bought a big pot of clivias in bloom at Gawler Railway Station market a month ago. Now, having moved clivias from the front garden which have been scorched there every summer, there is a beautiful green effect around the fig and plum. All I can think of now is how to buy more advanced clivias to extend the row right round to the apricot tree and then to reach the side fence.

Wednesday, 3 October

I have been planting dozens of rosemary prunings in pots to transplant later in the public garden I'm making opposite. Two have thrived there and now I see what a good plant it will be as it is so tough. I think of people walking home from work and being able to pick the herb for their lamb dinner. Thinking of this, it seemed that mint would be useful there, too, even though it needs a bit of water.

The small sick lemon tree I got from my neighbour Barbara's garden is now planted across the road and dying, I see, faster than it did in my garden. Jane, with whom I talk almost daily about our gardens, said there are plants that will not thrive and you might as well pull them out because they will never be any good. Thinking of that, I dug up the lemon and took it to find its fate across the road. I think it was the months of being unwatered in its pot that weakened it terminally.

Sometimes, it seems, watching a precious plant die that has had everything given to it, from Seasol, to water, mulch and much else, I stand there defeated, thinking, as it is possible to do about a person, too, 'Just die will you?' One more reason to join Montaigne in hoping that when death comes he finds me among my cabbages.

Speaking of cabbages, last week I ate the first of those grown around the cumquat's feet in the front which I had thought were Shirley poppies. It made a delicious meal for one with grilled chicken legs in honey, ginger and soy and oyster sauce. Daily I go out, pressing the heart of the next biggest cabbage. Two beetroot came in for dinner tonight to be grated raw with lime juice and honey for a salad to eat with chicken legs. Pulling beetroot from the earth is a pleasure that I can't comprehend. So little giving so much. For $5 at the supermarket I could buy a big bunch and while it would be pleasant to bring it home, it is nothing like harvesting your own.

I suppose this is why so many people are beginning to grow vegetables in places where lawns once grew or in above-ground beds or even on their balconies. It isn't that much money is saved, unless you are careful and frugal, sowing seeds yourself, making compost and using your own chicken manure or that of a friend's horse. A single vegetable plant at a nursery costs $4. Yet fully grown, that vegetable from a shop costs much the same and is probably bigger and, in the case of a cauliflower, whiter, too. Oh but the joy of it. It is better than cocktails. One of which I am now about to have. A new discovery: elderflower syrup, gin, lime and water.

Thursday, 4 October

'Get up and be happy,' I said out loud after lying reading on the bed in the sunroom all afternoon. And I was; gathering eleven eggs from the twelve hens and then hearing that a friend's mother who had dementia had finally died. A mercy. Now the radio is announcing that turmeric can help to avoid Alzheimer's disease. Pass the curry. There must be more to it than that. Turmeric, which came from a pot a friend gave me, grew in my last garden. For a long time I did not know what it was. Then I saw the rhizome but didn't use it as my son Hugh had not yet told me how keen he was on using it fresh from the greengrocer.

I am happy. Easier in acceptance, facing my fate, and grateful for all that has been given. As you see, time and the pills have worked. And when I look at the garden and at my life and how I spend the day, why wouldn't I be happy? Or is it all a matter of SAD effect, which one of my nieces tells me she suffers from. Seasonal Affective Disorder. In other words, is it just the arrival of spring? Maybe a bit of all.

Daily doing matron's round of the garden as if it were a ward, but unlike any matron, this is in my dressing gown with a cup of tea in hand, the garden in the early morning is soft. I pull weeds as I go, although I do not intend to as it slurps the tea into the saucer and spoils my nails.

Five rhubarb are doing well and now they have either parsley or chilli plants beside them for shelter, as I read in a magazine that it is what they like. Some sort of shelter from the sun. Anything will do, but not pure shade and they like a slightly acidic soil. So I have now scraped off the dolomite I threw around them.

Lime and dolomite have been poured onto the rose peonies that I have moved from the shade of the fig at the back to the side garden. They don't thrive in too much shade, the magazine said. I left one in the shade in case this move is not successful; I don't want to lose all five. Hedging my bets.

Ants ate Jane's peony in her first garden at Stirling, she says, so perhaps I should lay down some ant dust. She tried to grow a peony tree at Goodwood; even though she used ice cubes and it was a type bred for the plains, it died. We're mad to keep trying yet we can't seem to help ourselves; it has a challenge about it. A stand-off in the face of fate. We are willing to work for it. But I draw the line at ice cubes. If I get a peony to flower you will hear a shout go up even from inside of this closed book.

Friday, 5 October

The day of the clivias.

Louise offered clivias for the back garden to extend the edging of them inside the pink bricks. I took two trains to her home at Grange. We walked around her old house and garden which she and her husband have recently bought and she showed me the 'Black Boy' rose now trained up over a new shed and the 'Mutabilis' rose with which she is going to make a hedge. We had broad beans and small beetroot she has grown with a boiled egg and potato salad with mint, lime juice and olive oil I brought for lunch, and the only things that didn't come from our gardens were the potatoes and the oil.

Forty years ago, Louise did what was then an amazing thing. She made a hedge of white 'Iceberg' roses, half a kilometre long, for a hotel. It was the first time most of us had heard of these. They'd just been introduced.

Louise drove me home with bags of clivias and two bromeliads. Then she filled her bags with chicken manure that I dug out from the pen. As soon as Louise left, the clivias went into the ground under the fig, plum and apricot trees in the back. I hosed down the bricks and went to bed a happy wreck. I said to Hugh, who is a fit man, being a rower, that when I come home from a long ride or from working in the garden, I relish the moment entering the door if I can only just manage to push it open, trembling, because I know I have really had some exercise.

Thursday, 11 October

Strange weather.

It's been snowing in the hills and in the Barossa Valley at Pewsey

Vale; Mount Lofty and Belair have snow, too. My old friend Geoff Wilson is up at Belair on his own with a wood fire trying to paint a show of paintings for next year. Art takes grit.

The ground will now be cold and the 100,000 people I read of today who plant tomatoes in Adelaide and the suburbs will be glad if they have delayed the planting. The soil will now not be warm enough to sit on comfortably with your naked bottom, to test if it is safe to plant summer vegetables.

We have tomato fever here: the Dutch in the seventeenth century had tulip fever. It is our great topic. Next thing, tomatoes will be on the share market as tulip bulbs once were in the Netherlands. And speaking of tulips, the Dutchman Danny, who came and cleaned my windows, told me that when he and his family were starving in Holland during the Second World War, they had only tulips and sugarbeet to keep them alive. He said Sweden sent planes that dropped bread and butter and that was what saved some of the Dutch. I had wondered when I read in Antony Beevor's *The Second World War* if this was correct and coincidence has provided the living witness to the truth of it.

Now here's a thing. To protect the pots of herbs and flowers at the back door, I stuck prunings from the plum trees in the pots to keep the chooks away. Now the sticks have sprouted leaves. Naturally, I am thrilled. As soon as the cuttings are big enough, I will plant them in the new garden across the road and if they are not fertile it won't matter, because a tree is a tree is a tree and they are welcome here.

Speaking of fruit trees, today I bought a second blood orange. It can go down the side next to a lime near the back gate. Sheltered from the wind, it should thrive. For the first time in my life I stood at the nursery, looking at the tree in its pot and debating whether to buy it because I was wondering if I would live long enough to see it fruit. The other has done so well growing beside the side wall of the house, but would be destroyed if this house is bulldozed when I go. Everywhere here old houses go and two new joined ones are built. The trees that survive are those planted on the edge of the block and it may be that this second tree would have a chance against the side fence. Well, the tree came home in one of the panniers on the bike and I hope I see it fruit. Better, always, to say yes to life.

Saturday, 13 October

A breeding duck and drake are coming. Yes, Peter bought the pair for me at the Gawler market and the duck is laying. I have been longing for new life. Chickens or ducks, I don't mind. My red hens (ISA Browns) do not readily go broody, I am told, but the white ones do. Yet no white hen is sitting long hours on the nest so this is not the time to buy fertile eggs. Not being able to have a rooster in the suburbs, a drake is the solution.

I asked Peter if I could have his dog's kennel because his sheep dog, Fly, sleeps indoors nowadays. He said that I could have it, but a duck would prefer a piece of galvanised iron laid upright at an angle against the fence. The duck would make a nest in the shelter. I am looking for a baby's bathtub because ducks need a lot of water. They love to make mud and spend their days making it. I remember my mother saying that baby ducklings easily drown but I will face that later if I am lucky enough to have the need.

What I want now is a sheet of galvanised iron to prop against the fence, a bale of straw for the duck to make a nest inside it and a baby's bathtub. Also, bricks to prop up that iron and to lead up to the water and make a stand in the bath so that ducklings can rest on it while learning to swim. And what Peter needs to do is first catch the ducks which are not tame and are in with his forty chooks and to bring me, if he can, all the other things. Thank God for brothers. Peri and I may feel, as you know, that we may have knitted nettle jackets for our brothers but mine do help me. Nobody but siblings remember each other as infants. For example, when Peter was a baby and I was six, I used to take him daily around the block in my doll's pram after breakfast while our parents washed the breakfast dishes.

Monday, 15 October

Riding to Peter's to give him the weekend papers, I met him in his four-wheel drive coming to see me. He didn't say anything. We went back and he carried in a box and some wooden-framed net fences. I peered into the box and beheld a duck and a drake. Mallards. The duck is already laying, he said. As they were tipped out of the box, they ran into the shelter of a tree in the corner, full of darkness. They are shy. I asked why and he said, 'That's how mallards are, but they will settle down.' This gnomic stuff that comes from farmers.

I ran around like a headless chook and gushed with gratitude. I would've considered knitting a nettle vest. Peter set to and a fence went up with a little gate for me to access the chook pen and the ducks. A piece of galvanised iron was propped with bricks and star pickets against the back fence, then stuffed with hay for a nest. He put down two bowls, one with a brick in it for water and the other for food. Barely a word had been said. He came indoors, drank a cup of tea and ran his fury about the government past me, and left.

spring

Monday, 22 October

The curtain went up on a gold, silver and black sky this morning. The tall pine is black against the silver sky and the new leaves of a gum tree are gold in the early light. I lie in bed and take my fill.

I now have ducks. It is like keeping a pair of unicorns in the garden. They slide in and out of the shade like shadows of a myth. Although they are shy creatures, if I am quiet and move slowly, daily they grow more trusting and are willing occasionally to come out into the light. For example, the drake is now sitting in the water bowl grooming while the duck sits beside on the gravel with her head tucked under a wing; a family portrait. Had I known how easy ducks are to keep, I would have had them long ago. So far, no eggs laid, although, as you know, Peter said that the duck was laying when he bought them. The shock of their move here may mean it will take a while to resume.

Yesterday eleven friends came to lunch under the vine. At dusk as the people stood up to leave, the drake strode up to the duck, mounted her and, after a wobble, mated with her in a spectacular end to the party. It was a heartening sign for me as it may mean ducklings will come.

Tuesday, 23 October

Two duck eggs buried in hay, under the sheet of galvanised iron that Peter propped up for their shelter.

Wednesday, 24 October

I see now that I was wrong thinking the duck had her head tucked under a wing while sleeping beside the water bowl. Geoffrey Chaucer says in *The Canterbury Tales* (1386) ' . . . small fowles . . . slepen at the night with open ye [eye]'.

In *Bird Sense* (Bloomsbury, 2012), Tim Birkhead says that song-birds, ducks, falcons and gulls can sleep with one eye open:

> One-eyed sleep is easiest to see in ducks roosting during the day beside urban ponds: with its head turned back towards the wing (often incorrectly described as 'with its head under its wing'), the bird has one eye facing inwards towards its back and concealed, the other eye looking outwards and opening from time to time. (page 30)

What a coincidence that having written about the duck sleeping with her head under her wing, the next day I should read that this is not correct. The author goes on to say that in a study of mallard ducks, which is what these are, those sleeping in the centre of a flock spent less time sleeping with one eye open than those on the edge, where it is safer to keep one eye open for predators. And this is where we get the saying that sometimes a person is 'sleeping with one eye open'. Or that someone is 'keeping an eye out for trouble'.

This is a gripping book. I do long to know what my poultry see and feel. And if you believe they do not think, when the chooks crowd at their gate hustling towards me, it is hard not to believe they are full of longing to be out scratching under the fruit trees. Then when I come out towards them as they flutter in their dust baths in a quite ecstatic way, they reluctantly stand and head back towards the pen in a group: obedient as soldiers. I used to stamp and make bossy sounds until I saw how startled they looked and what an unpleasant interruption it made to a happy time. So I stopped that. I've learnt I must make a certain call, such as 'Come on!' Or I bend over to get a stick to herd them and so stop them from making a dash back to the garden. It is the bending down, too, that tells them it is time to go. Tomorrow I will listen to the noise I make and report it to you.

Saturday, 27 October

I celebrated too soon. When I came home yesterday afternoon and peered inside the shelter where the duck's nest is, the two eggs the duck had laid then buried in the straw had gone. No broken eggs, because there was not a sign left of shell or yolk. A mystery. With my hands I dug around wildly down to earth and gravel but there was nothing there.

Grinding my teeth with the mad disappointment, I came indoors and made some phone calls. We have no possums here, as far as I know, so it's not that. Peter said that had it been a rat, it would have eaten the eggs in the nest and there would be remnants. There is nobody who would steal the eggs and the duck can't carry them away in her beak to another nest if she made one. There are times with nature where you just have to shake your head and try again. I could scream.

Packing chook eggs this morning I noticed how similar to duck eggs were two of the white hens' eggs. I have put them in the nest to encourage the duck. It's dusk now and there has not been a duck egg laid last night or today.

Yet something was achieved, because at Bunnings nursery I found two eggplant seedlings on sale for a dollar each. I bought them along with cucumber seeds. They are all planted out the front now, beside the olive trees where the cabbages grew a week ago. Two cabbages were big enough to make coleslaw but the other ten or more were pulled out; too small for anything except chook food.

Tuesday, 30 October

Heat is coming. It's due to be 33 degrees and soon I am riding down to have the first swim of the season. All the 'Little Gem' lettuces, beetroot and the two eggplants will have a hard time of it. I have put upturned buckets over some plants and the rest must live or die.

The ducks have an upturned bin lid filled with water with a brick in it under the apricot tree and they love it. The duck was missing yesterday and today but appeared later so I think she was in the nest. But no egg yet. Those two lost eggs were more precious than pearls to me.

Magpies have been carolling daily on top of a Stobie pole near the back gate. Tim Birkhead says that their singing is antiphonal—'an alternating duet so beautifully synchronised that it sounds like a single bird . . . [it] consists of the entire magpie group—some six to eight birds—standing on the ground, often around a bush or fence post, and together uttering their haunting melodic song.' (page 201) A magpie carolling researcher, Ellie Brown, Birkhead says, has found 'Communal songs, like motets and madrigals, are made up of the combined melodies of all the singers'. When you consider the intelligence of a human choir required to sing a madrigal, it seems reasonable to think that birds are clever.

Now I have found what it is that makes my hens run back into their pen. I say, 'Come on!' Then, 'Shoo!' Shoo!' and sometimes, if they seem reluctant, I bend down, pick up a stick and, with that, they rise from their dust bowls, or from scratching the big roots of the plum tree (which they have now exposed like plumbing) and run as a troupe, back to the pen. This means, surely, that they understand the meaning of some human sounds. Then, when a hen has laid an egg, the sound made tells me, indoors, what has happened. So I, too, understand some poultry sounds. Pretty soon, if this continues, these chooks and I will write a book.

Later; it is dusk and the air is cooler. Now here's a thing: Joe, Nora's son, who has come to live next door with her, came to the place where a side fence would be if we had one and said, 'There's a problem.'

I walked towards him with that grim feeling which comes when you know somebody has power and you have lost some of yours.

Joe said, 'It's your ducks. They make a noise. They peck the fence all night. They are probably looking for insects. It's very loud.'

I apologised and said, 'I will ask my brother to make a barrier to keep them away from the fence.'

Joe was smoking as he spoke so I said, 'I have a problem also, Joe, because I am asthmatic I have difficulty with your smoking.'

He said, 'I'm asthmatic, too.'

We left it at that. I went out to the ducks and built a palisade of old mirrors, wire and watering cans to keep them from the fence. I wait to hear from Joe if he can now sleep.

Wednesday, 31 October

Dozens of newspapers on which the chooks roost have not dissolved where they were laid as mulch. Today I ran the mower over them and made a snowstorm in the street. I had no idea that papers already soaked in buckets of water would be difficult to make meld into the soil. It was a heady business and now I see, as never before, how rough the garden looked with rolls of paper under every bush and tree. These things happen slowly like the body ageing, as I've said, and it is not until something wakes you up that you realise what has been happening while you were blithely living life; blind to what is often obvious to others.

It reminds me of something my friend Babs Pak Poy said years ago, 'If it crosses your mind in the morning that your hair might need washing and you decide against it, before evening you will dearly wish you had.'

The same can be applied, Jane and I have found, to the thought that some man or other seems to fancy you. Telling yourself you are being stupid is a mistake. If you think it, you will later find, when certain events take place, how right you were. Whether you wished it or not. In other words, if the thought crosses your mind, believe it.

Bathers drying in the plum tree. After the mowing, covered in dust, I rode down to the sea and was the only one in the water. There are cold showers along the esplanade and, as cars whiz past, you can shampoo your hair there while you shower, so I did and rode home in wet bathers. The pleasure of these childhood things.

Thursday, 1 November

The day of the cucumber. Determined to have apple cucumbers this year, I sowed half a packet of seeds. They are in the front and side of the garden along with a dozen seeds of a long-type green cucumber from the time when I couldn't find the apple ones. If you add grated drained apple cucumbers into cream, with a little vinegar added, it makes a salad or sauce that is good with fish. My mother made this as well as 'Iceberg' lettuce salad sliced finely with a dressing of mashed hard-boiled eggs, salt and pepper, vinegar, mustard and cream.

One forkful of these and I am at our wooden table on a hot night, eating cold lamb with my three brothers and parents. We have been swimming after school, our noses are sunburnt and peeling as they seemed to be the whole long summer. No wonder I am wrinkled. Four white-haired children on a blazing white beach. Our father was called Snow Brinkworth and his lips were often sunburnt after auctioneering sheep in a town far away.

Now it is plain, after re-reading articles on tomato growing, that they must have no fertiliser at all until flowering time. I piled up soil around one to make it able to send out roots from the main stem. Odd to think that, when I knew nothing of these matters, the first crop here was stupendous. The plants simply lay and spread like green lions on the mulch and withstood tremendous heat. I can't remember watering them but I must have. They had no wilt or rust or virus or wooden stakes or burning, although the water would have been poured on in my ignorance.

Now the mystery of the duck. Day after day in the morning the drake is alone. Full of faith, I believe the duck has gone to the nest to lay. When, later, I look in the nest, there is no egg so I make the story that the duck is practising and will soon begin again as she did lay two eggs soon after arriving. Today, the duck being late, I worried that a fox had come and taken her so went to the nest and found it empty except for the hen's egg remaining. So, where was the duck? I looked everywhere and this yard is not big. Nowhere to be found.

Then later when I had begun to think the worst, she appeared with the drake, eating lettuce. The only place the duck could be is behind the new water tank where there is a tap which I now can't reach. If she is laying there, what is she laying the eggs on? If eggs are to hatch they need straw or material that will keep them warm. There is nothing there, I think, but cement. Do ducks drag in straw and make a nest? Heaven knows. I need a small child like a chimney sweep to crawl in behind the tank and investigate. I need Gianlucca and Gulio, those two little boys who came to lunch a fortnight ago. On that day I gave the children a white rabbit Peter had brought me. I wanted to introduce them to pets. They took it home on trial. When I asked them to name it, Gianlucca said, 'Bob.' If the elder can't fit, the younger may.

These are beautiful days, full of meaning over the most trivial but profound things. To grow plants and have creatures to mate and multiply is joyous and calming. No matter how agitated I get, the effect is still full of verve and meaning.

'What do you want from your life?' I once asked a professor of English with whom I was having an affair.

'Point,' he said.

Point? What's point? Well, here is my point. It will do. My children are away and I can't make a difference to their lives except to love them. The same with their children. Although, with them, I can teach them things and philosophise and make memories. But in the here and now, under my nose, what I have is life. It may not care for me but I care for it and that, perhaps, is the secret.

Friday, 2 November

A coup! Yes, seven duck eggs hidden among the mint bushes. All this time while I have been bemoaning the loss of those two duck eggs, this has been happening. I saw a dark shape in the mint and wondered what this shadow could be. It was the duck, snuggled into a small shape, deeply asleep. She looked dead and, as this was hours later than when she usually appears, I floated some straw down to see if she was alive, but there was no movement. An hour later, finding her the same, I touched one of her feathers and she woke with a jolt then went straight back to sleep. Maybe she is broody already. I hope not, I'd like the chance of more ducklings. Never satisfied, you could say.

But while Cyclone Sandy is tearing at New York and other places, all I need is what I heard yesterday: that two of my darlings who are there are safe. We are all treading water until we die and can only hope to find things to love and to help to grow and to be loved, too.

Sunday, 4 November

We shall see now what this little mallard duck is made of. The question is, will the duck stand over the eggs if it gets any hotter than it is today, which is 36 degrees? She is definitely broody as she is sitting on the nest all day, only coming off at dusk for a short time. I never had such swift success. One week there was a duck and drake here and within a fortnight, the duck was sitting on her seven eggs. This business is engrossing. If it is this easy, and certainly I am counting ducklings too early, I would like more ducks from which to breed. But, while the duck is sitting, I won't buy more as strangers could upset her.

This process is like a human pregnancy as the date counting has begun. But I am not yet sure how long duck eggs take to hatch. If a hen takes twenty-one days, perhaps a duck would take twenty-five. I will ask around. The question is, when did the duck actually begin sitting on the eggs?

In the meantime, while all this preposterous fuss is going on, plants are lying dying across the road where I meant to plant them. Aloes are tough and so are some nameless bulbs. I plan to be working over there tomorrow. No hose will reach that far, therefore buckets are needed and it is that which makes me hesitate.

Monday, 5 November

The first gardenia bloomed this morning. I brought the flower indoors to sit in a saucer of water to sniff as I cook. Having killed three gardenias in pots as I fed them too much liquid chicken manure, it's clear now that some should be transplanted into fresh unpolluted potting mix. There's an element of shame in killing a plant that you wanted to thrive, even if it was done with ardour.

It's hot, with a few drops of rain and thunder. I have tried to protect the duck and the nest from getting wet by erecting a bin lid balanced on a watering can with two towels on top.

Today, twenty 'Roma' tomato seedlings were planted from my seed boxes. I am optimistic as these plants all went into soil that had not grown tomatoes before. The great thing is to pile up soil around the stem as they grow so that they can make more roots, spreading out from what will be the trunk of the plant.

It is seven in the evening and the duck has finally come from the nest to drink with the drake. Calculating the hatching, if it is to be, from the day the duck was missing and must have been sitting on the nest she made in the mint bushes, Friday, 23 November, will be twenty-one days. When I asked Peter this morning how long duck eggs take to hatch, he said that it varies with the type of duck.

Muscovy ducks, he said, take the longest time. Therefore, because these mallards are about the same size as a chicken, I calculate a similar time for these eggs to hatch.

Tuesday, 6 November

It is traditional that tomato seedlings should be planted out on Melbourne Cup Day and this is it. By coincidence, as I was dragging a dying, metre-high gardenia plant from its pot this afternoon, a bright red tomato appeared from a self-sown plant beside it. This shows that gardening rules depend on weather. The back pots, you see, have sun many days in winter and it was the warmth that made that tomato. It is for dinner with a whole fresh flathead, tzatziki from a cucumber I was given and couscous with salted lemons which I preserved.

Today I took Jane two jars of them as her tree isn't loaded. Never willing to try to grow a lemon as there have been too many failures, limes are the tree I grow. Nora from next door and another neighbour give me plenty of lemons. These trees of theirs, as far as I can see, get not a jot of care and are abundant in huge fruit. It may be because the trees are old, fifty years or so. But I know that dead branches should be removed so as I pick these beautiful scented heavy lemons, I break off a few dead boughs as I go as a kindness to the tree.

Thursday, 8 November

Yesterday the local paper reminded people that it is the time to bury a lamb's liver under their passionfruit vine. Thinking the butcher would have sold out, I was glad to be able to buy one. Then

I remembered how delicious lamb's fry is so I cut some for myself and had it fried with onions for lunch after the main part was dug in beside the passionfruit. To stop a dog digging there, I put a heavy broken pottery dish on top and covered that with mulch.

The chook I had buried beside the 'Granny Smith' apple near the passionfruit was dug up soon afterwards. When I saw the red feathers on the path and in the gutter, I thought a fox must have raided the pen. I counted the hens, and sure enough, one was missing. For days after that they were locked inside the shed, not just in their yard. But later, I realised it was feathers from the chook which had been buried, not feathers from the living. Having recounted, I found there were the dozen still present.

Peter had his appendix out today. This is unusual in a man of his age. There was no food left for my poultry and Peter could not bring any, so Lindy drove me to Oliver's produce store to buy it. We bought plants there, too. I priced baby duckling food, although not prepared to tempt fate by buying any. Much can go amiss. The duck can abandon the nest, rats or crows can take the young, the eggs may not all be fertile, a heatwave could interfere with the hatching and so on. Such a simple thing, common even, and yet here it will be a red letter day if ducklings hatch.

Saturday, 10 November

A fine day. Lindy and I walked by the sea hoping for dolphins, but as she said, there were too many yachts out. We saw plenty of shell grit which would have been good for the chooks as it makes their egg shells stronger. We are going back with bags to bring it home next week and hope the tide has left some. Eleven eggs from the hens, including one the size of a pigeon's. Perhaps it is a pigeon's egg. No hen, even as a pullet, laid an egg so small. If it is not a pigeon's, it could be the Murray magpie's, as lately one has been here daily. Yesterday it flew into this house. Having half-knocked itself out on the windows, when I shooed it out through the door I saw it had soiled the quilt in the back bedroom which is washed now and drying on the fence.

Yesterday, seeing a punnet of healthy 'Rouge Marmara' tomatoes on sale for $1, I bought them and planted them where the cabbages grew. There will be a tremendous harvest if all this planting works. Yet I hesitate to think it as I don't want to be bold and feel I was a fool if it all comes to nothing much. Growing vegetables is as unreliable as horse racing.

Speaking of horse racing, I see the drake is on his own most of the time, looking in the mirror I propped up against the iron fence to stop the noise of pecking that bothered Joe. Bart Cummings, the horse trainer, has a mirror in every horse's stall because, he said, horses are group animals and it may make a horse which is alone in a stable feel calmer if it can see another.

So Mr Drake sees another all day long and, at first, pecked the other in a friendly way but, as he has never had anything except the same response, has given up. The duck comes off the nest to drink in the warm hours of the day; yesterday, at about eleven in the morning; today, at three in the afternoon. She dunks herself over and over in the deepest of the water bowls and quickly returns to the nest. When I took food out, she lowered her head as I neared the nest and made a short run at me to defend the nest. This is a good sign.

Monday, 12 November

Across the road in the new garden, I was planting five lemon-scented gums Helen gave me which, with luck, will grow to 30 metres, when another young woman spoke to me and said, 'I've been wondering who's been making this garden. I wonder if you'd like some cactus?' I said yes, although cactus has never had any charm for me. But it shows that the changes here, however small, are being enjoyed.

'You can say what you like about Balts, but they are very clean people.' This, from my mother when displaced persons, as they were known, fleeing after the Second World War, came knocking on the farmhouse door asking to rent two stone sheds. My mother said that the sheds were not fit for people but the two men who came said that they were better than the sheds in which they were living. So Olga and Maria came with their husbands, Peteris and his friend whose name I forget. The women helped my mother in the house to help pay their rent.

Monday was washing day. Olga and Maria turned out to be such brilliant laundresses, rinsing everything thrice, that my mother was won over.

This was the age of the copper, a huge pot in which clothes were boiled. Then, with a copper-stick (a long thick piece of wood), the clothes were lifted out into the washing machine and from that into a tub of cold rain water, then lifted into another tub, drained and put into a final rinse of water turned blue from a cube of Reckitt's Blue to whiten the linen. The clothes were then turned through a hand-driven wringer comprising two wooden rollers, put into baskets, taken to the clothesline which was propped up with tall wooden sticks, pegged on and hung there in the sun until dry.

The washing was then brought indoors in wicker baskets and dampened with water flung on lightly to soften it (our mother did this by dipping her fingers in water), folded and left ready to be ironed next day. If you think making a car is complicated and hard work, try washing clothes in those days.

The song 'I've Come to See Georgina' is not too far off the mark:

I've come to see Georgina, Georgina, Georgina,
She's up the stairs washing and you can't see her today.
I've come to see Georgina, Georgina,
She's up the stairs folding, folding and you can't see her today.
I've come to see Georgina, Georgina,
She's up the stairs ironing, ironing and you can't see her today.
I've come to see Georgina, Georgina,
She's up the stairs airing, airing and you can't see her today.
I've come to see Georgina, Georgina, Georgina,
She's up the stairs dead sir, dead sir and you can't see her today.

I asked Hugh to help me check the words of the song and he said, 'You used to sing that to us. It's a melancholy song.'

I remembered this and wished I had remembered that children are affected by these old dark songs. The song 'Old Father Thames', learnt at school, was a blow to me when we sang, 'What does it care for you or me?'

Yesterday was Remembrance Day. I walked on the beach gathering two bags of shell grit at eleven o'clock, the silent minute. Reading Antony Beevor's *The Second World War*, as I said last month, reminded me of those two families who came to the farm, had their babies in the local hospital, later bought homes and settled in. Lucky there were stone sheds on that farm.

Tuesday, 13 November

Today I made a swimming pool for ducklings, if they hatch. To save the ducklings from drowning I used an old electric frying pan with gravel in it and a piece of broken pot to make a ramp up to the side. I quizzed Peter about breeding, if there are ducklings. Should another drake be introduced as this one would be their father?

'Yes. But why breed more?'

'Well, Paula says the eggs are good for cake making.'

'You don't need a drake to make a duck lay.'

That's true. This would mean the drake would have to go (otherwise he could mate with his progeny) and the duck would stay. Seems hard. I think ducks, like swans and geese, mate for life. If you want to wrangle with ethics, rear creatures.

Now in a phone call I've been told that drakes kill ducklings. Whatever next?

Wednesday, 14 November

This afternoon, a man from the council was spraying poison onto weeds on the garden I'm making across the road there. When I went out to soak a pot of succulents to transplant them, I saw him. I ran over and said that I was making a garden there. He'd been told this a few months ago but he persists in the spraying, all the while under his wide white cloth hat; ruthless and courteous. Like the best kind of bureaucrat it took Kafka to describe. With a rising feeling of defeat, before beginning, I said, 'Look! Here is a rosemary, this is a brugmansia and here's another rosemary.'

He pointed out that the thistles had thorns and were a problem because they could travel and get into gardens.

In a beaten way, with an arch of an arm, I pointed to the wild green weeds only a metre away from us, growing inside the railway line fence.

'Well, what about those?'

He didn't reply but said that I could put a bucket over the brugmansia to protect it from the spray. I told the man that I had weeded there. I do sometimes take thistles when I have no greenery for the chooks or am planting there. He said that these prickly thistles needed special gloves if I were to pull them out. The jonquil leaves, aloes and the nameless bulbs still green were glistening with spray.

Defeated, I turned away and said, 'Oh, this is ridiculous!' And began to walk away.

Looking down, stepping onto the road, I saw I was wearing only a camisole over trousers as I had been lying reading when it had occurred to me that the succulents needed watering.

The man said again, 'Well, these thistles will need gloves if you are going to pull them out. I'll tell the council that you'll take care of it.'

Friday, 16 November

There is a bag of two dozen eggs, cumquat chutney, three 'Little Gem' lettuces, limes, a bunch of lemon thyme, other herbs, red chilli, round carrots and one parsnip pulled this morning to go in my case to take to Sydney to have an early Christmas with my son and his family. Slowly, while a person is gardening off and on, the plants spread and suddenly it comes as a shock to see that there is a small crop.

A bit wilted myself after the visit of the poisoner, I took buckets of water over the road yesterday and poured it on whatever still grew. There are three brugmansias left and that is better than none. There are about a dozen cuttings ready in the seed boxes to be planted so when I come home I will do it.

The great thing I learnt when making a railway station garden with my friend David at Woonona was to begin again immediately workers have dug up the garden. To just plug on. In one part of that garden it was dug up seven times and seven times we went back. The trees are beautiful now. Some were lost naturally, and not all of those that died were killed. Some were not suited to the place; they needed more water than we could get them with our barrows and buckets. Though the Chilean pink-flowering tree that Peri bought from the Botanical Gardens in Sydney has survived and it is a mighty and beautiful thing with its trunk of thorns.

Wednesday, 21 November

Home from Sydney and the duck is still sitting and, if nothing disturbs her and if the eggs are fertile, with a new calculation there may be ducklings on or about the 30th of this month. At a dusk picnic on Monday, I asked Ghil'ad, the father of those two children who came and played with the chooks, if they would like a duckling each for Christmas. He looked startled and said that the family were flying to Israel the next day. I, too, was startled at this news, as war there seems imminent. Later, I realised that people are likely to be optimistic and just hope things will take a turn for the better, especially when going home and their plans have been made long ago. In fact, Ghil'ad was bringing Bob the rabbit back that day. The family is leaving briefly, for Ghil'ad to teach in Israel. He's the new professor of linguistics here and is rescuing our dying Aboriginal languages.

While New York has had storms and snow, my family tell me they are safe there. It is not always the way that an entire state is wrecked, even if on television it looks as if it is. I have a fancy for those children to have a pet duck each. Hearing from Ghil'ard that the family won't be back until February means the ducklings would be safer to leave with their mother until they're three months old.

'Quality Ageing' is the headline in *The Adelaide Review* in an article about Adelaide's Thinker in Residence, Professor Alexandre Kalache, who says: 'If we start thinking about what we can do about this Longevity Revolution—the fact that we have another thirty years to live compared to previous generations—we can figure out how to make those extra years meaningful and not seen as a burden.'

The doctor says that training for medical professionals means that they are learning everything about child health when they will likely be dealing with older patients more and more. If you don't have the knowledge in that area, you're more likely to make mistakes.

It sounded as though the geriatric would be treated by paediatricians. In her old age to keep dementia away Doris Lessing learnt Russian.

Pressing on, the doctor said, lack of sunshine and therefore vitamin D is directly linked to dementia. I was smug thinking I had enough of this vitamin until the test was done. Truly astonished to find, in spite of swimming and beach walking, like millions of others, I was deficient. Calcium can only be absorbed with enough vitamin D and even though Jane and I stuff ourselves with cheese and drink Milo, we both needed to take it in pill form.

Stephanie is on the Paleolithic Diet which excludes dairy food and said, when I asked where her calcium comes from: 'Oh, there is plenty of calcium in green-leaved vegetables.'

'Not enough, my darling, not enough,' I thought but didn't say.

Yesterday I saw a health poster that said also being deficient in vitamin D can be a precursor to cancer.

Thursday, 22 November

A few nights ago I began to worry about how the chooks will treat the ducklings if they hatch. I asked Peter, but he was sanguine and said that they would be alright. But he doesn't care as much as I do, having reared hundreds of ducks himself. He bred so many that he filled a tall freezer in his shed with their six-month-old bodies that he had dressed. When I proudly asked him to show Shirley, that late negative friend of mine, the freezer full of ducks he had reared, killed and dressed, he flung open the door. She said, 'Oh, what if the power goes off?' He is still getting over it.

He sold a lot of ducklings for $8 each to the feed shop where he buys the food for our poultry. They sold them as pets for children, which is how I got the idea of Gianlucca and Gulio having one each if my lot hatch.

When I first came here, I performed what I did not know is called 'trench composting' by digging in waste food around the roots of trees. Although there were no crows to be seen, they flew in within an hour or less and began to dig up the food. They especially like meat. Because I didn't want to encourage them with their melancholy cries, I put the food into the tumbling, rotating compost bin.

This may sound strange, but I believe that crows have a sense of humour. I'm backed up by an article I read today in the December 2012 issue of *Gardening Australia* that crows have been seen playing pranks with domestic animals. Other research studies have shown that crows and other birds are as intelligent as chimpanzees.

Well, I'll tell you.

On Peri's farm there was a crow plague because fertiliser from the cane fields had run into the rivers and killed millions of fish that lay dead on the sand; the crows ate the fish and multiplied. During a visit, I saw a murder of crows hanging around in the garden by the verandah where I lay. All were standing around on the lawn when one crow walked over to a plant about a metre and a half high, with a thick strong trunk, and began to climb up the trunk and to fall down, wings flailing. There was no fruit on the plant, the crow could have simply landed on a small branch had it wanted to search for fruit. It simply repeated the trick. The others watched while the crow performed this trick again and again. It was like a clown's act and, watching closely, I couldn't think of any other reason for the crow to do this unless it was showing off and intending to amuse the others. Like all comedians, the crow would have gained status within the group by being funny so it was worthwhile. But sometimes, there is no reason for humour but just the pleasure of it. So I have seen a crow clown. And here's the thing: I found it funny, too.

In the night I worry, as I said, how the chooks will treat the ducklings if they come. They have had two almighty fights with the drake when he was trapped in the walkway to their pen and shed. They share the water bowls and the area under the apricot tree.

But these hens have never seen a duckling. Peter, the font of much of my poultry knowledge, keeps saying they will probably be okay. That's not good enough for me.

What if a hen, feeling threatened, attacks a duckling? I have been thinking of how they could be separated until they become used to the ducklings. This, all the while in a manner that would allow the chooks to come out daily from their pen as they do now. I decided that a barrier needs to be made which will keep the hens down the alley way leading to their shed and pen. It is cemented there so they would need, not only a barrier, but a bale of hay spread for them in which to scratch. They would miss out on dust baths until things settle down. But that's the price of new life.

I took the wheelbarrow today to a street rubbish dump I saw when riding past. Brown wooden doors were piled on each other. One is now here and, laid on its side edge, will make a barrier between the poultry until it is safe to let them mingle. I can open it wide enough to get through to bring in food and water.

Saturday, 24 November

It's been hot today and the chooks dug under the apricot tree down into the cool dirt. They lay there, half buried, in ecstasy. The green cave of vine outside the back door is a miracle. It gives a green light into the back room where I read. It's wonderful how fast and thickly it grew. These glory vines are thicker and quicker than fruiting grape-vines, I now know. Therefore, I've changed my mind, and in another house would do what I earlier regretted here and plant the glory vines.

Spring

When I was married and lived in Dulwich, Adelaide, we wanted a vine to shade the back of our house. Opposite us, an Italian family grew grapes, made their own wine in a bathtub near the back door and grew much of their own food on the block they owned beside their house. It happened that the government of the time announced that a road would be made which would come right through their home. Mr C, who had come from Sicily and had built all this, had a nervous breakdown. He went quietly mad.

But just before his final collapse, I found that he had a mature vine shading the back of the house that he had dug out. He said, when I asked, that I could have it and should bury the trunk, which went up to the gutter of his house, along with the surprisingly small root ball, all together in a trench. I got the vine home, perhaps with his help; I can't remember. Then with my husband watching, because he could not do it, being in a wheelchair, I dug a shallow trench. I was so pathetic that Richard said, 'I can't bear it. Turn me around.' So I did.

Then Great-uncle Stanley, an eighty-year-old World War One veteran, arrived for a visit. Grasping the situation, he took the spade and began to dig. No doubt it brought back memories. You could call it the blind helping the blind, but we managed to get that vine's trunk and its roots laid horizontally with a few branches and leaves above the trench at one end. This was the most marvellous vine and for the fourteen years we lived there it gave shade every summer and washing baskets full of grapes, too.

This gave me the belief that if you just begin something, even if it seems beyond your strength or ability, plug on because the great thing is to begin. Somebody will help you.

Tuesday, 27 November

It's hot today. On Thursday, the day before the eggs are due to hatch, 40 degrees is expected. Hanging wet towels over the upturned chair above the duck on the nest today may have helped. I thought of it in the night. When it is hotter I will run a lead through the laundry window and turn on an electric fan beside the nest. Those eggs are not going to overheat even if I have to stand there all day with an ostrich fan.

It's dusk now and the duck is drinking at the water bowl, having floated around in a deeper bowl. She groomed herself while the drake groomed nearby. I wondered if it was a bonding process, much as people sit matching each other's hand and leg movements while talking, mostly unaware of what they are doing.

Peter and Helen's house is on the market because they've bought one in Glenelg. More tomatoes were planted at Peter's yesterday and I got another punnet for one dollar today to add to them. I am keen to have a crop of red tomatoes before that house is sold. And, if it sells before the tomatoes are ripe, the new owners can have the pleasure and it may even swing the sale of the house seeing a sensational crop. You do not know what makes people want to buy a house. It is not always as logical as we may think.

For instance, I got a house because I wanted to learn how to make pastry and in the kitchen there was a long bench of old white marble. That did it. I told Grandfather Llewellyn that was the house I wanted. So he bid for it and got it. Luckily the house had a lot of other attributes which proved more useful.

Thursday, 29 November

Ducklings.

spring

It happened that when Joanie came to take me to lunch, I showed her the nest and the cooling system I had rigged up with four wet towels draped over the watering can, a bucket and the upturned chair under which the duck sat among the mint. An electric fan blew on the duck from a lead from the laundry window. I saw two broken egg shells beside the duck and thought that if she hadn't eaten the contents, as that hen did long ago, it may mean success. We went to lunch then drove to Oliver's and bought baby chicken food as they had none left of their game bird chick food. When we got home, lifting the layer of towels, there was a flash of yellow beside the duck. Two black and yellow ducklings lay asleep beside the mother. Still on the nest, the duck sat like a rock.

Friday, 30 November

As I walked out of the back door this morning, the duck was standing under the apricot tree with something flickering around her legs. I thought the movement might be a sparrow, but looking closer, saw two ducklings. Then more and more emerged, a sea of babies. A flood of joy made me put my hands to my face over and over and then put them together. 'This is joy,' I thought. There were so many ducklings, I could not count them among the morning shadows as they are dark with yellow breasts and tiny black bills.

Off and on all day I have watched the antics of this crew and tried to count them. There are nine or ten. Thinking the duck had laid seven eggs, to find this merry crowd is miraculous. The ducklings eat the food Joanie and I bought yesterday. They drink often, swim in an upturned bin lid, sliding in and climbing out easily. When I first saw them, I ran inside and got saucers and bowls of my mother's glory box Royal Doulton for water, fearing they might drown in something deeper. These 1930s designs have wide, shallow soup bowls. I didn't care about the recklessness. Anything to keep these little creatures alive. They swim easily and do not lack confidence. When I next eat an egg I will pay more respect.

The mother stands above them when they rest and widens her wings over them and they disappear for a short time. The drake has paid no attention to this event, although he may have been humming to himself after this long celibacy. And longer to go, too, I imagine, as the duck cannot lay eggs until the ducklings are safe to leave.

When I went for a swim later, I thought, looking down at seaweed, if a shark were to take me now, I would die happy. I rang Peter to thank him for bringing me the pair of ducks and to tell him the news. He was impressed with the number, as I hoped he would be but did not expect. I said, 'Do you think they will drown? I can remember Muttee said that ducklings can drown.'

'They only drown if they can't get out.'

Oh, I see.

These creatures emerge from an egg able to walk, swim, eat, forage, preen, freeze if the mother does, then move when she moves, sleep beneath her, jump up and down on bricks, and are full of verve and delight. They are not anxious. In the night they must sleep ten hours or more, wake and begin to eat. It is six in the afternoon and the ducklings are back in the water. They are not yet a day old. If one were to die in the night, I would be sorry, but not grieve because it has had a perfect day.

If you want to be happy and if you have a few metres of earth, breed ducks.

Spring

Now, at six-thirty, all have gone to rest. So it may be that they sleep eleven hours a night. The mother duck, with a heart-shaped blaze on her breast, seems to be breathing at the same rate that I am. She has been shuffling around above the ducklings and each time she settles, one or more of the ducklings seem to ruffle things below. Then the duck rises, breathes deeply, and lowers herself onto the brood again. Night approaches. May there be no foxes.

Summer

Saturday, 1 December

At seven this morning, the duck stood up from her brood and they emerged sleepily, like children from their cots. They did not eat, but when they had woken, after a minute or two, went straight to the water bowl and drank. There are not nine, but ten. All day yesterday I tried to count them but, with their movement, I could not.

Today the ducklings have spread out more from the mother, whereas before, in their first hours of life, they kept beside her. Duck, drake and ducklings all love to eat lettuce leaves.

Planting cosmos seedlings in the front garden today, I saw that some lettuces have begun to go to seed. It's the heat. In the *Organic Gardener* magazine I read that lettuce needs shadecloth in hot weather or it will bolt and grow bitter. And this is what has happened. Better to pick them young, even too early, than to wait.

Tuesday, 4 December

It rained in the night. Only softly now, it is a cold day. Pouring liquid manure on tomato plants this morning, even though the advice is to give nothing until flowers appear, the wind was sharp.

The duck stands over her progeny and they shelter there then rush out and jump into the water bowls. This means the day can't be too cold for them.

In Murray Bail's book *The Voyage* (Text, 2012), a Dutchman travelling by ship with the narrator says:

We should not be disapproving of repetition. Each day we see the same things, eyes, noses and legs, the trees and clouds, and each day we repeat the same words. And we never stop doing the same things over and over again, every day, sleeping, cleaning our teeth, shaking hands, drinking tea, sitting on a chair, which give stability to our lives. It is necessary. Daily repetitions form part of what we call love.' (page 86)

Counting eggs, tomato and basil plants, ducklings, and all that is growing here seems trivial yet I have pleasure from it. I do it again and again. It could be that I have a touch of Asperger syndrome which runs in the family.

Have you noticed, that when an individual has a certain mental disability or ability, their siblings can have a featherlike touch of the same; hardly noticeable, but on a closer look it becomes clear?

Here are some numbers I counted today. There are eight drakes among this hatching and two ducks. The imbalance may be related to the hot weather the eggs endured or perhaps it is the time of the year. Yet this can't be normal. Mallard ducks are easy to sort, having black backs and black legs, while the drakes have orange legs and brown speckled backs. Even at five days old their gender is clear. No ignominious sexing by a professional chicken sexer is needed.

Now, going out to empty the teapot, I see the ducklings putting their beaks into an empty food tub and, as you know, my motto is 'None shall hunger'. I have thrown a handful of baby chicken food towards them while the mother hissed at me. Her motto is 'None shall come near'. Even as I pour buckets of shining water into the water bowls to which the whole family rush as if in a desert, the duck hisses. There will be no compromise. She will not relent. This means I am always in the role of intruder while being, all the while, provider. Some husbands, I suspect, feel like this.

Wednesday, 5 December

It was a chilli day of cayenne pepper and dried chilli flakes. Joanie told me that cayenne pepper sprinkled onto the edge of garden beds will deter blackbirds from digging up plants. I poured the pepper from a big packet onto the pink bricks beside the vegetable garden. I am making four trays of chilli and nigella seed cheese biscuits to take to Peri's husband Bob in Sydney. I sneezed for an hour because I threw cayenne pepper over them as they went into the oven, having forgotten to put chilli flakes into the mixture. These are delicious little biscuits and he has one with a martini at dusk, which is now, at eighty-five, his only drink of the day. And now, to mine.

Thursday, 6 December

Last night Peter told me that I cannot keep a dozen ducks in this small backyard.

When he heard of two ducks and eight drakes, he said he had never heard of such a thing and all his ducklings are roughly 50 per cent of both genders.

The smell of a dozen will be a problem and there won't be enough room for them to roam. He's right. I have been avoiding thinking of what will become of this lot.

The drakes are to be sold as children's pets. Luckily, it is almost Christmas. The dealer does not want to keep ducklings that do not sell early because they are a problem for him as they age. But he will take these and those that are not sold, I will welcome back and find something else to do with them. If that sounds sinister, perhaps it is.

Tuesday, 11 December

More heat. This morning I ladled out liquid manure onto tomatoes, zinnias, cosmos, cucumbers, rhubarb and beans. 'Take a risk,' I said, because it was black and strong and could burn the plants, but tonight I see nothing has withered.

The ducklings have more than doubled in size. They are frisking in the water every hour but do not enter any of the water bowls if the drake bathes there. If their mother occupies it, they dive merrily in and out. I throw their food beside the roasting dish that holds water and retreat as the duck hisses, lowering her head, showing her pretty pink tongue. There is a ritual: eat, drink, swim, preen in the sun, sleep and repeat. Not unlike me.

Wednesday, 12 December

Too hot to swim. It's 39 degrees. The hens pant and lie in straw under the fig outside the kitchen window. I hosed them down to their surprise so they fled squawking into their shed. Doing the same to the ducks, wetting the soil under the apricot tree, they did not care for it, either. I walked back to the tap to turn the hose off and hosed myself down, too. Then I walked back into my own shed, the bedroom, and lay in front of a fan.

I feel sorry for any creature that cannot read. They must lie passing the time by blinking. Albert Camus's mother was illiterate and in his posthumously published autobiography he said his mother told him that, because she could not read, she had to lie on her bed and wait for him. What an imprisonment.

I noticed recently that when I meet a friend whom I have not seen for some years, to see how well they are ageing I listen to how often they repeat themselves and how much they talk about themselves. Also, how far they are willing to walk. For instance, if we are shopping or going to a restaurant, do they want to take a taxi?

Because it becomes a habit to lean forward and take small steps, a friend told me to lean back and take bigger ones, and it does help. An elderly bachelor friend, who is in frail health, said that he told the district nurse when she had come to visit that he was embarrassed to be incontinent and wearing nappies. She said, 'Don't worry, Mr X. Half of the city is in nappies.'

Saturday, 15 December

Yesterday morning it poured with rain. The ducklings sheltered from it under the apricot tree right back against the fence. When the rain stopped, they emerged and rushed to dabble their beaks in little runnels in the gravel. The truth has dawned and now I know there are too many ducks for this small backyard. It is only 5 metres from the door to the fence and I am worried that, as they grow, they will upset the neighbours with the smell.

Silent, happy little creatures, only the mother quacks occasionally as I bring fresh water or food. I never saw anything grow as fast as these. It must be because they are a wild breed and need to be able to fly as soon as possible. They stand upright like cormorants after swimming and wave their miniscule wings in the air to dry. It is not easy to stop watching and, as I watch, I feel the trap tightening around me. They just must go. Peter says he'll come to take them to his dealer to sell as Christmas pets for children, but he is busy.

I greeted them with such ecstasy.

Now with every day that passes the ducklings become less cute and therefore less appealing as pets. Add to that, it is only two weeks till Christmas so you can see the need for haste.

CHRISTMAS POEM (4)

We are looking for an angel
in any form at all.
Rustle, rustle go the leaves
as the rain falls down—
the wonder of water
after it being so long dry—

Twelve ducks (ten ducklings
and their parents) play in their water bowls

under the laden plum tree—
If you want to see an ordinary miracle,
watch a duckling hatch.

Sorrow and dread began and ended this year
all the gifts of Christmas.
Yet, love, trust, hope, faith and strength
are what the angel meant
with that great star it shed leading on
while we follow; some halt, some lame,
and those whose knees
or hips grind in agony
along with all our dancing children
their grace, our blessing.

'Even a live dog' Ecclesiastes says
'is better off than a dead lion.'
So what's a walking stick or wheelchair
when you're still alive and lucid
and outside, the moon, the stars
and somewhere among them
the angel with the news.

Thursday, 20 December

This morning, Peter caught the eight drake ducklings and took them to his poultry dealer. They were hard to catch. I had a broom to push them up into a corner. Peter got down low, spread his arms and legs and swooped. Twice he got a female and, cursing, put her down. Then quickly he gathered three drakes at a time. It is lucky the genders are easily seen.

I bent to see, for the last time, the little drakes' bobbing heads in the box covered with wire netting. It was not hard to see them off because they could not all live here.

The mother still has two to care for, so perhaps will not mourn the others much. The father will have more room now, in the roasting dish where he loves to swim.

Roland, my neighbour across the road, came over when I asked if he would care for the poultry while I am away for four days at Christmas. He asked if he needed a pen and notebook but I said it was all pretty straightforward.

Friday, 21 December

It was more straightforward than I had imagined. As I walked out this morning, there were no fleeting shadows under the apricot tree. Pouring out food to bring the ducks increased the stillness. 'They must have got out,' was the first thought. Slowly, as if I already knew, I realised there was no life at all. Gone. Then I saw the mother's feathers on the ground and knew. It seemed incredible luck that those eight drakes had got away only hours before.

I walked around the garden and saw more feathers on the front lawn.

When the ducklings hatched, I wrote that even if they died that evening, they had had a perfect day. And now that is what I think.

Whatever the parents' lives had been before they came here, they lived an idyll for those weeks and fulfilled their lives breeding so many ducklings.

I rang Peter and told him. I asked if it could have been a dog, but he said it would have been a fox. Now the chooks must be locked in their shed every night. It is good luck, too, that they were not taken as a fox will often kill every bird even if it can't eat them all.

Sunday, 23 December

Today I came south on a hot and crowded bus to spend Christmas with Tucker and the family. Patricia met me at the Henry Creek Road turn-off and, as the driver pulled my case from under the bus, thanked him. We drove through their wetlands and paddocks with deer hiding in scrub. Black Angus cattle stood in shade if they could find it. We drove in the gates and past an avenue of old pines. Screaming out from the pines came a flock of black yellow-tailed cockatoos. They flew off over a shearing shed. We passed a small lake and a bronze sculpture of a life-size bronze Murray Grey bull among gum trees, and up the driveway to the sprawling house.

I am to sleep in Tucker's shed as all the beds in the house will be taken by others due here soon. In a room with fifty or so heads of stags, two wild boar and one goat on the wall, the single bed Patricia had made up for me stood with a green and pink floral patchwork quilt with white sheets. The feminine and the masculine.

Bookshelves to the ceiling on one wall hold some of Tucker's books. I had a good snoop. He favours biographies of famous men; books on Africa, military history and others by ecological writers. I saw that he has all of Antony Beevor's books, which is a pity because I had bought him *Stalingrad* for Christmas. Piles of opera records were on a table beside the leather couch with a green woollen rug and cushion where he rests after lunch. He was out fighting a bush-fire and would be home for dinner later.

In *The Second World War*, Antony Beevor writes, 'Moral choice is the fundamental element in human drama, because it lies at the very heart of humanity itself.' (Weidenfeld and Nicolson, 2012, page 782) As this visit progressed, I was to think of this often.

Patricia went out at dusk to feed the dogs and the white Muscovy ducks. I went, too. A duck had four yellow ducklings, hatched today, out on a pond. Two more ducklings were in the nest and about a dozen eggs. Two of the eggs had beak marks where the duckling had begun to break out. I wanted to go in and open those shells and bring out the ducklings towards the mother but Patricia said to leave them alone. The yard has had a fine wire roof put on, as dozens of ducklings have been taken by crows. Or else snakes or rats have come in through the fences.

'Every day, one less,' Patricia said. 'And I am sick of it. So I got the men to make it safe.'

There were five other Muscovy ducks sitting on eggs in an empty water tank cut in halves. Another sat in a box with no base or lid from which ducklings will not be able to move so that nest must be watched and lifted up and away as soon as the eggs hatch. Talk about ducks galore. From a tank hung high up fell a mixture of grains onto the ground when Patricia pulled on a rope. 'This is all our grain,' she said.

A small caramel and white Jack Russell has had four puppies a month ago and they are now fed small bits of mince meat along with their mother's milk. We walked back to the house, watching the smoke from the bushfire rising into the clouds.

My brother came in from the fire, took a bath and sat down with us to a corned beef dinner of one of his cattle. Earlier I'd been shown the beef lying in a bath-sized plastic container of brine in a cold room. After dinner I went back to my land of happy stags and slept like a lion among them.

Monday, 24 December

Early this morning, down near the pale silver lake, the sound of the dogs, barking like the hunters they were bred to be, showed that they had probably caught a snake.

Patricia and I were drinking tea in her kitchen and, hearing the noise, she said, 'Oh, if those dogs have got a snake, it could kill the puppies' mother and they'll have no more milk!'

We ran down to the lake, with me being warned not to go near the fight.

No amount of calling could bring the dogs away so, after a while, Patricia walked back to the house, warning me again not to go too close. I went slowly towards the clump of bamboo where they had something bailed up. It was a fox, snarling and injured, unable to get away. The dogs kept trying to bite the fox and it kept trying to defend itself but was bleeding from one hip.

Walking back up the driveway to the house, having seen that it was a fox, I suddenly thought that it ought to be put out of its misery. Then the thought came to me that perhaps there was a little sliver of cruelty in this, because a fox had taken my ducks. The mind is cunning like a fox.

However, it was clear that the creature would suffer for hours because the dogs would not let it go and it would be tormented until it died. So I took one of the spades from a door on the verandah where they are kept in case a snake comes and walked back.

It is not easy to kill a fox. It was like killing Rasputin. Even unconscious after a blow to the head, it kept breathing. I took a spade full of black mud from the edge of the lake where it lay and tried to smother it. A soft wind blew its fur and beneath were respirations, slow and continual. More mud. More rising and falling of the chest. There is a time during a killing when horror rises while you know it is too late to stop. Eventually when I thought it never would, the fox died. It took more than one blow to sever the head of Mary Queen of Scots and many more to kill this fox. Violence is never pure and rarely are the motives for it. Already, I was questioning myself. On a farm, a woman usually has a man to ask to kill something so we are not used to it. But we can do the deed.

I walked back to the verandah with Patricia's pink velvet dressing gown and my white socks soaked with black mud. I told her it was a fox with mange and that I had killed it.

She said, with a piercing look, 'Oh, take off your clothes, you have to have a bath and I'll wash your clothes. People can get mange, too, you know! And now I'll have to treat the dogs because they've probably got it and they'll give it to the puppies. I'll have to get a man to bury the fox where it can't be dug up.'

Later this morning I pruned the lavender. Tucker had gone out early to check on the fire and when he came back at lunchtime he said the fire was out. It had been caused by a spark from some farmer's pump that had dry grass left around it.

Tuesday, 25 December

Happy Christmas. Silence. A still day, not hot. I wandered around among the stag heads and into the other room that has African buffalo heads and an alligator skin on the floor. I'd like to have got on with this day, but everyone was asleep. Defeated, after testing every door on the main house, I came back to the shed for more tea, got back into bed and read more of Tucker's copy of Clarissa Dickson Wright's *Rifling Through My Drawers*. (I'd brought Vassily Grossman's *Life and Fate* to the farm but even though it's a masterpiece on the Second World War, it was too tough for me at this time.)

Tucker came into his kitchen and I walked out to greet him. He wished me happy Christmas. He had boiled one of their big ducks the day before which he'd corned earlier along with a big piece of beef. I couldn't imagine that corned Muscovy duck could be very nice but held my tongue. It's been a long time since he put his new little Christmas hammer into the top of my Christmas doll's head.

Cars pulled up in the drive, everybody appeared at once. They carried presents into the living room where the decorated tree stood. Lucy showed us a diamond and announced that she was engaged to Kato. We drank to them. Then a frenzy of present opening. The excitement and kindness. The tradition and pleasure. For how long we will be together, nobody knows. 'We are all looking at the wrong one,' as my friend Clare says when somebody is frail. Everything is fragile and needs to be treasured for that moment. Nothing lasts, although we act as if it will.

Outside, cattle chewed their cud as they do at that time of day. Deer sheltered among the scrub on the low hilltops while the ducks sat on their eggs and ducklings floated on the pond.

Above, the pale arching sky sheltered everything as the black cockatoos rested in the pine trees.

We went in to lunch. Ben was carving at the kitchen bench. We took our plates into the dining room and three generations sat down, waiting to begin to eat the food they had grown.

Annabel said grace.